CW00549673

1

INTRODUCTION

Welcome to the world of Fibonacci trading, where the art of technical analysis meets the precision of mathematical ratios. In this book, we embark on a journey of discovery, uncovering the secrets and strategies that revolve around Fibonacci analysis—a powerful tool used by traders worldwide.

Chapter 1: Unveiling the Foundation of Fibonacci In our opening chapter, we delve into the core of Fibonacci analysis, unraveling the fundamentals that underpin this technique. We'll explore the concept of Fibonacci retracement ratios, a key element in understanding price retracements and reversals.

Chapter 2: Exploring the Essential Requirement for Accurate Trend Identification Accurate trend identification is paramount in successful trading. In Chapter 2, we delve deep into the essential requirements for precisely identifying trends, laying the groundwork for effective Fibonacci analysis.

Chapter 3: The Depth of Fibonacci Retracement Values Building on our foundation, we delve further into Fibonacci retracement values. Understanding the depth of these values is crucial for making informed trading decisions.

Chapter 4: Uncovering the Essence of Fibonacci Projection Values Chapter 4 takes us on a journey to uncover the essence of Fibonacci projection values. These values provide insights into potential price extensions, a valuable tool for traders seeking to project future price movements.

Chapter 5: The Power of Fibonacci Convergence Fibonacci convergence is a concept that can significantly enhance your trading strategies. In this chapter, we explore how the convergence of Fibonacci ratios can be a powerful tool in identifying key reversal points in the market.

Chapter 6: Ideal Time to Open a Position Timing is everything in trading. Chapter 6 guides you through the ideal timing for opening positions, helping you make strategic entries into the market.

Chapter 7: How to Optimize the Trade Entry Optimizing your trade entry is a critical aspect of successful trading. In this chapter, we provide insights into refining your entry points and discuss the flexibility of stop-loss levels.

Chapter 8: The Art of Exiting a Trade Exiting a trade is as important as entering one. Chapter 8 explores the art of trade exit strategies, helping you make informed decisions about when to close positions.

Chapter 9: A Great Combination of Fibonacci and Elliott Waves We delve into the synergy of Fibonacci and Elliott Waves in Chapter 9. This powerful combination can provide a deeper understanding of market dynamics and enhance your trading strategies.

Chapter 10: Secrets of Better Trade Management Effective trade management is key to long-term success. Chapter 10 reveals the secrets of better trade management, helping you maximize your profits while minimizing risks.

Chapter 11: Big Mistakes That May Cost You a Lot of Money Mistakes in trading can be costly. Chapter 11 highlights common errors that traders make and offers insights on how to avoid them.

Chapter 12: Powerful Fibonacci Tools in Real Trades In our final chapter, we demonstrate the practical application of Fibonacci tools in real trades, providing you with tangible examples of how to use these techniques effectively.

Conclusion We conclude our journey through the world of Fibonacci trading, summarizing key takeaways and leaving you with a deeper understanding of this powerful approach to the markets.

"Vivienne Elara: The Author Behind the Book

Vivienne Elara is more than just a name on the cover of this book; she is the passionate and visionary mind behind this work. Hailing from the United Kingdom, Vivienne has harbored a deep-seated passion for the world of finance and investments since her youth, immersing herself in books that told stories of evolving markets, growing economies, and investment opportunities.

Under the pseudonym Vivienne Elara, she began to create not love stories, but extraordinary financial strategies, market trend analyses, and approaches to investment portfolios. Her guidance doesn't come from academic titles but from her insatiable curiosity and strategic vision, which have given life to worlds and characters that resonate with investors worldwide.

Each of her works is a tribute to the power of economics, with engaging plots, captivating characters, and indelible moments that capture readers from the very first page. Her books, including the acclaimed "Investing in Challenging Times," have become pillars in the world of finance and investments.

Outside the pages of her books, Vivienne finds inspiration in the surrounding nature and everyday life, residing in a charming village in Sussex. She is not just an author; she is a dreamer, a passionate investor, and a true lover of economics in all its facets. With this book, she continues to share her passion and enlighten readers with her unique perspective."

Prologue

In this literary undertaking, I shall unveil the essential instruments employed by traders of all levels in their pursuit of trading success – the Fibonacci retracements and extensions. Forged from the timeless foundation of numerical sequences, these tools serve as unwavering mirrors, reflecting the intricate tapestry of market psychology. They will illuminate a new pathway for identifying critical levels within the market, eliminating the uncertainty that often shrouds the initiation and conclusion of price fluctuations. If you find yourself vexed by consecutive trading losses, this compendium may offer the solutions you seek, along with the remedies to rectify them.

With years of traversing the trading landscape, my dedication has been committed to sharing my strategies, particularly with those new to the world of trading. My enduring fascination has consistently revolved around the analysis of price dynamics and trends. Among the multitude of tools available on trading platforms, none have captivated my attention quite like Fibonacci. At its core, "Fibonacci" is simply a method of employing numerical patterns in your trading decisions. Though it may initially appear intricate, rest assured that we will demystify its complexities.

These tools have steadfastly formed the foundation of my trading strategies for over a decade, spanning across various asset classes, including stocks, forex, commodities, and the ever-evolving realm of cryptocurrency trading. My objective is to illuminate the formidable potential of these instruments and impart the correct approach to harnessing their power. As you conclude the final chapter of this compendium, you will be equipped with effective strategies that can be applied to a wide array of assets, whether your focus lies in the short or long term.

As the wise Warren Buffet professes, "The most important investment you can make is in yourself." Without consistently adapting your approach and effectively deciphering the intricacies of the market, achieving longevity in this pursuit remains an elusive goal. Failing to approach the market armed with the fundamental knowledge of Fibonacci tools can lead to the unwarranted depletion of your hard-earned capital. For newcomers to the trading world, understanding the fundamental market principles embedded in Fibonacci tools is the linchpin that can help you avoid unnecessary losses on your trading journey.

The tools presented in this compendium have been empirically proven to generate remarkable trading signals and deliver outstanding results for traders of all types. Each chapter within this opus is intricately interlinked, dissecting techniques through the lens of crucial price action elements on the chart. Notably, candlestick patterns take center stage, providing you with a reliable compass for navigating the markets, while avoiding the complexity of convoluted indicators that can consume both time and resources.

Furthermore, you will unlock the secrets of trading confluence, an asset in various scenarios, and understand why confirmation signals are essential when selecting an entry point. The importance of cultivating a mindset conducive to success will also be revealed. As you reach the conclusion of this compendium, you will have achieved mastery over the indispensable tools that will accompany you throughout your enduring journey in the world of trading.

CHAPTER 1: UNVEILING THE FOUNDATION OF FIBONACCI

Drawing from the mathematical underpinnings of the Fibonacci series, Fibonacci analysis possesses the unique capability to anticipate the magnitude of price fluctuations, whether upward or downward, within the intricate tapestry of financial markets. It stands as one of the select tools capable of forecasting price levels in advance of actual market movements. The utility of Fibonacci analysis derives from its proficiency in pinpointing critical support and resistance levels, thus furnishing traders with valuable insights to guide their buy and sell decisions.

The advantage of Fibonacci over lagging indicators

+ How most indicators perform

The majority of trading platforms abound with a plethora of indicators that traders often depend on to inform their trading decisions, guided by visual cues. While these indicators can be incredibly valuable, it's important to recognize that each of them has its own set of limitations.

In essence, many technical indicators operate by scrutinizing past market behaviors and then applying mathematical algorithms to historical data, ultimately generating visual signals that serve as guideposts for traders in their decision-making process. These indicators fall into a category known as "lagging indicators," a term aptly coined to signify their reliance on analyzing previous price movements. Consequently, these indicators tend to furnish traders with feedback that lags behind the current market conditions.

Common examples of lagging indicators include moving averages (MA), moving average convergence divergence (MACD), relative strength index (RSI), and stochastic oscillators. While these tools can provide valuable insights into market trends and potential reversal points, it's crucial for traders to be aware of their inherent lag and limitations when employing them in their trading strategies.

+ The power of Fibonacci

Indeed, the strength of Fibonacci analysis does not stem from a straightforward mathematical formula where you input numbers and receive an immediate, definitive answer. Instead, its power lies in its predictive nature, classifying it as a leading indicator within the realm of trading tools. Fibonacci tools are adept at discerning potential support and resistance levels before the price actually reaches them.

Leading indicators, such as Fibonacci, bestow traders with the ability to anticipate future price movements, thereby enabling them to potentially initiate trades at the inception of a market movement. However, it's important to recognize that while Fibonacci tools are potent, relying solely on them may not yield consistent long-term profits. Achieving reliability with these tools often necessitates their integration with other analytical techniques, including a keen focus on price action, and adherence to a stringent set of trade management rules. These aspects will be explored further in subsequent sections of this book.

Where do Fibonacci numbers come from?

Leonardo Pisano Bogollo, famously known as Leonardo Fibonacci, introduced the Fibonacci series to the Western world during the 13th century. This numerical sequence possesses remarkable mathematical properties and ratios that can be observed not only in nature, historical artifacts, and biology but also in financial markets. It's one of the key reasons why many investors employ Fibonacci analysis to identify significant turning points in price charts.

To understand the Fibonacci sequence, we start with the numbers zero and one. Subsequently, we add the two preceding numbers to obtain the next number in the sequence, creating an infinite progression, as follows:

0, 1, 1, 2, 3, 5, 8, 13, 21, 34, 55, 89, 144, 233, 377, 610, 987...

For instance, the number 3 is the sum of the previous two numbers, 2 and 1.

This is the origin of the Fibonacci sequence, where each Fibonacci number occupies a specific position in the series. The sequence serves as the foundation for calculating Fibonacci ratios, such as retracements and extensions, which will be detailed in subsequent chapters.

The Fibonacci sequence and the related ratios and proportions have found application in various facets of the natural world. However, you might wonder how this connects to financial markets. Markets essentially consist of individuals making their own investment decisions. Yet, when you gather a multitude of people all observing the same market performance, you can observe common emotions, shared psychology, and similar reactions, all of which influence market dynamics. These collective responses and their resulting market outcomes provide another realm where the application of Fibonacci analysis proves valuable.

Fibonacci retracement ratios

Simply put, Fibonacci retracement ratios are used to determine where the price may revert after a swing, facilitating a trade entry.

For example, in an uptrend, the Fibonacci retracements are placed from the major low of a swing to the major high of the swing, generating a series of price levels which may act as potential support on any retracement/correction from the prior swing.

The principle is similar to a downtrend, only differing in which such levels are used to look for potential resistance.

There are some noticeable connections between these numbers that create the basis of Fibonacci trading. While we cannot cover every connection in this chapter, some listed ratios below are the most important retracement levels you should be aware of.

- If you divide a number by the following number, it will work out to approximately 0.618. This figure is the basis for the 61.8 percent Fibonacci retracement level.

- If you divide a number by the second number after it, it will work out to approximately 0.382. This figure is the basis for the 38.2 percent Fibonacci retracement level.

- If you divide a number by the third number after it, it will work out to approximately 0.236. This figure is the basis for the 23.6 percent Fibonacci retracement level.

If you have seen Fibonacci retracements on a trading chart or have read about Fibonacci retracements, you have probably seen some additional levels which are, in nature, not derived from Fibonacci ratios. The midway marker, or the 50 percent retracement is a typical example of this. The 50 percent level has a psychological impact on the chart. This is where the markets often react, hence this level is usually used by traders.

Another popular level which does not come from Fibonacci sequence is 78.6 percent. Adding this level to the Fibonacci retracements brings about a sense of balance with the 50 percent marker in the middle, two levels above and two below. Moreover, although it is not originally derived from the Fibonacci sequence, the value of 0.786 is the square root of 0.618, which is one interesting aspect to look at.

The 78.6 percent line is the deepest retracement level. Traders will analyze carefully the potential of a reversal when the price corrects to that point.

Now we have the most important levels used in Fibonacci retracement: 23.6 percent, 38.2 percent, 50 percent, 61.8 percent, and 78.6 percent.

Fibonacci extension/expansions ratios

Fibonacci extensions, also known as expansions, exhibit similarities to Fibonacci retracements in their utilization of Fibonacci ratios to pinpoint potential price reversal zones. Nevertheless, their primary function revolves around assessing the impulse waves that follow a retracement within the overarching trend. These tools extend beyond previous swing points to delineate levels of support or resistance, providing traders with valuable insights for identifying exit points for their existing positions. We will delve deeper into the crucial distinction between Fibonacci extensions and Fibonacci expansions in Chapter 4.

Now, let's return to the intriguing Fibonacci sequence:

0, 1, 1, 2, 3, 5, 8, 13, 21, 34, 55, 89, 144, 233, 377, 610, 987...

Recall the process of calculating retracement ratios by dividing a number by its subsequent number(s). When dealing with extension levels, the procedure is reversed. As we progress through the sequence, dividing a number by the one preceding it yields specific ratios. For instance, dividing 89 by 55 results in a ratio of approximately 1.618.

Moreover, dividing a number by two positions to the left yields a ratio of approximately 2.618. Similarly, dividing a number by three positions to the left yields a ratio of approximately 4.236.

Much like retracement levels, extensions encompass two "unofficial" levels: 100 percent and 200 percent. While not inherent to the Fibonacci sequence itself, these levels represent points where traders' psychological reactions tend to manifest. As a result, these levels can carry significance in the analysis and decision-making processes within the realm of financial markets.

Fibonacci golden ratio

As mentioned above, any number in the series (excluding the first few ones) divided by the previous one will work out to around 1.618. This is known as the Fibonacci golden ratio. For Fibonacci traders, the golden ratio and the inverse of it (0.618) are what they pay most of their attention to when looking for an entry as well as an exit level.

Other Fibonacci tools

You may have heard of other available Fibonacci trading tools, and be wondering why I don't mention them in this book.

A short answer is because my trading plan is based on retracements and extensions, and to me, they are enough for executing successful trades.

I won't say that other tools are not worth trying. In fact, some traders are still using Fibonacci fans, time zones, or arcs as the core of their system. You may try these out at some time during your trading career. If you ask for my advice, I would recommend you master retracements and extensions first before using the others.

The application of Fibonacci retracements and extensions strategies

Fibonacci retracements and extensions work in both an uptrend and a downtrend. While I try to cover strategies in both directions in this book, there are certain cases when I use an uptrend as an example. In such a case, please keep in mind that things work similarly in a downtrend.

For example: If I suggest placing a long order if the price **breaks above** the 50 simple moving average (SMA) in an uptrend, you can infer that a short order can be placed if the price **breaks below** the 50 SMA in a downtrend.

CHAPTER 2: EXPLORING THE ESSENTIAL REQUIREMENT FOR ACCURATE TREND IDENTIFICATION

Before we learn how to draw and analyze the Fibonacci retracements and extensions effectively, let's first talk about "the trend" because it is the pillar in building success in Fibonacci trading.

A trend is the general direction of the price of any asset over a certain period. There are two types of trending markets: uptrend (also a bullish trend or upward trend) and downtrend (also a bearish trend or downward trend). When there is no trend, we call it a sideways market (range-bound market or ranging market).

The key to successful trading with Fibonacci is to trade in the direction of the overall trend.

It sounds simple, but it is not always easy to define the correct direction of the trend. In other words, determining a trend goes well beyond what's apparent at any moment.

It is necessary to open a position in the right direction to generate profits. If the trend is up and you go short, chances are that you will end with a loss. Incorrectly determining a trend may lead to a disastrous outcome.

Three types of market behaviors

Now, let's dig deeper into these three types of market behaviors as well as some reliable methods of identifying a trend.

+ Sideways market

A sideways market (range-bound market or ranging market) has no discernable upward or downward price trend. In a sideways market, prices move in a range, changing direction multiple times before a clear trend forms and develops.

Statistics show that the price trends 30 percent of the time and moves in ranges for the remaining 70 percent. Sideways markets can be very frustrating for traders. In this type of market, a trader needs to be patient until there are signals that the sideways period is over and the market is clearly trending up or down. Let's look at a range-bound market below:

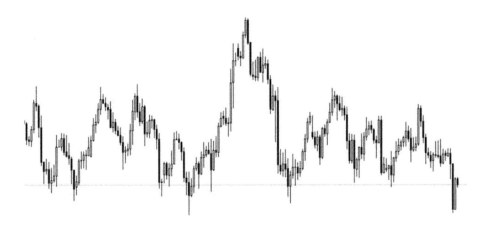

Trading in a range-bound market can be tough. Without a clear trend to jump on to, it is difficult to determine good entry and exit points, leading to potentially disastrous losses. For most traders, it is advisable to stay away from a ranging market.

+ Trending markets

The opposite of a sideways market is a trending market, including uptrend and downtrend.

13

Notice that in any trading chart, you will probably see that prices **don't go in a straight line in any direction, but rather in a series of highs and lows.**

Let's talk about the uptrend. An **uptrend** shows a general upward movement in price, composed of higher highs and higher lows. Take a look at the example below:

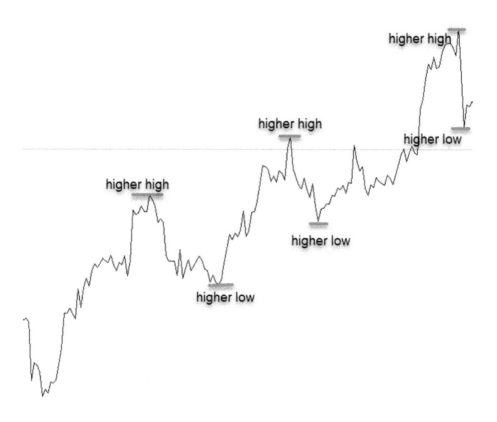

In a downtrend, the prices create lower highs and lower lows. Again, let's take a look at a typical downtrend below:

14

Determining the major highs and major lows plays a crucial part in drawing Fibonacci retracements and extensions, which I will cover in detail later.

Remember that in some unusual cases, the price may go straight up or down. This happens mostly when some unexpected news is causing panic or euphoria among traders. It may look promising on the chart; however, trading in those situations is super risky.

Another way to identify a trend

Technical analysis tools can be used to identify the current trend of the market. One of the most popular indicators used by many experienced traders is the simple moving average (SMA), i.e., the 200 SMA. When the price is above the 200 SMA, consider taking or remaining in your long position. Otherwise, you should look for a short position.

Which moving average is used depends greatly on the taste of the trader. Some traders may prefer the 200 SMA while others pay attention to the 50 SMA or 30 SMA. There is no fixed suggestion as to which SMA should be used.

16

My favorite set of moving averages:

In order to confirm the market trend, I prefer a set of shorter moving averages as below:

- The 20 linear weighted moving average (20 LMA)
- The 35 linear weighted moving average (35 LMA)
- The 50 linear weighted moving average (50 LMA)

The principle: If the 20 LMA is above both the 35 LMA and the 50 LMA, and the 35 LMA is in the middle, then the trend is probably bullish. In this case, I look for a long entry. This is illustrated in the picture below.

If the 20 LMA is below both the 35 LMA and the 50 LMA, and the 35 LMA is in the middle, then the bears are probably taking control. In this case, I look for a short entry. Let's take a look at the chart below.

If the moving averages are mixed and do not fall into any of the conditions above, I may use other tools to look for help, or just wait until a clear direction appears.

The importance of a longer time frame

Now you have some background regarding how to identify the current trend. If there is a trend in place, and you identify it successfully, you are halfway to a good trade.

Determining a trend is of prime importance. Yet it may be difficult for traders because sometimes the chart gives you nothing but turbulence. In these cases, you should **switch to a longer time frame** to have a clearer picture of the market.

Whenever you are confused about the trend, watch it at a longer time frame. In the one-hour chart below, you may think that it is a range-bound market.

To verify it, look at the four-hour time frame below.

Now you should be more confident to confirm that the trend is bullish.

Let's move to some other examples where you can see why signals from a longer time frame are so beneficial.

Below is the one-hour chart depicting the Australian and US dollar (AUD/USD) currency pair.

Things seemed favorable for a short entry, where the price almost retraced at the 50 percent level after a downward swing.

To verify, let's switch to a longer time frame. Below is the four-hour chart on the same pair.

As you can see, things are much different on the four-hour chart. Going short might put you in jeopardy because the underlying trend was bullish. The seeming downtrend that we saw on the one-hour chart was merely part of a correction.

22

There are some technical implications here with Fibonacci levels drawn on the chart that may create some confusion to you as a trader. Don't worry; they will be described in detail in the next chapters. The above pictures are just to illustrate the idea that a longer time frame will better assist you with identifying a market trend.

CHAPTER 3: THE DEPTH OF FIBONACCI RETRACEMENT VALUES

The use of Fibonacci retracements

Fibonacci retracement levels are mainly used to determine support and resistance levels. At some time, the market's supply and demand correlation may change, and the dominant side may lose its steam on the way. The market may witness certain pullbacks before continuing its overall trend.

In an uptrend, you could go long (buy) on a correction down to a key support level, whereas in a downtrend, you might look for a short (sell) position when the price corrects up to one of the key resistance levels.

How to draw the retracement levels?

So far, we've shown that in a trending market, the price rarely goes straight up or down. In fact, its moves often serve to create higher highs and higher lows, or vice versa.

In other words, the price moves in zigzag shapes, often known as swings or waves. Drawing the Fibonacci retracement levels on the trading chart requires clear knowledge about the swing high and swing low.

First, we need to identify a swing move in the direction of the overall trend (from A to B). After the main swing, there should be a correction in the opposite direction to point C. Point C should locate between points A and B. On a chart illustrating an uptrend, it may look like this:

Below are four essential steps to draw Fibonacci retracements correctly:

- Identify if there is a clear market structure (big zigzag shapes).
- Identify the overall trend (up or down).
- Determine the recent major swing high and major swing low.
- Connect the two extreme points A & B (from highest to lowest during a downtrend, and from lowest to highest during an uptrend).

Let's look at the Fibonacci retracements drawn on an upward chart.

Should the price touch the retracement level?

Some traders may have their preferred levels that they think the market often retraces to, such as the 61.8 percent or 38.2 percent of the prior swing. Their experience with many trades and trends may cause them to use these levels rigidly. However, the retracement may be a little bit shallower or deeper than the exact Fibonacci level, and it is still a valid move.

We should all be prepared for those times in order to not miss good opportunities.

Take a look at the US dollar/Swiss franc (USD/CHF) chart below.

We can see that there was a dominant downtrend. Then came the correction, where the price looked as if it would touch the 61.8 percent retracement level, but it did not. However, it was still a valid correction. After the retracement, the price strongly bounced back to its original trend.

Fibonacci retracement levels between 0 percent and 100 percent

As I mentioned earlier, using some of the most common Fibonacci retracement levels is more than enough. I won't say that other levels are useless or not working effectively. You can use more levels, but at the beginning stage, you may want to keep it simple and base your decisions on some of the levels shown below.

Over time, when you gain more experience, you will decide which are the most important ones and which ones you prefer to use.

Accordingly, take these levels into account:

- **23.6 percent**
- **38.2 percent**
- **50 percent**
- **61.8 percent**
- **78.6 percent**

Using Fibonacci to define the strength of the market

From my experience, the shallower the retracements are, the stronger the overall trend is.

A shallow pullback often appears around the 23.6 percent and 38.2 percent levels. Understandably, shallow pullbacks are typically seen within a **highly** trending market. When a market is moving strongly in one direction, we often do not see enough support behind the countermove. In other words, although the dominant side is losing steam, the counter side is not strong enough to make a considerable correction. The trend is, therefore, highly likely to continue in its underlying direction.

With that said, we cannot deny the fact that a retracement to the 61.8 percent (or even 78.6 percent line) may still trigger a very strong trend later.

Watch shallow retracements closely because chances are you may ride a strong trend later on. With a very strong trend and a shallow retracement (such as 23.6 percent or 38.2 percent), you can look for some ways of entering a trade that will reduce the likelihood of major losses. We'll go into these in detail in Chapter 6 and Chapter 7.

Take a look at the GBP/JPY chart below.

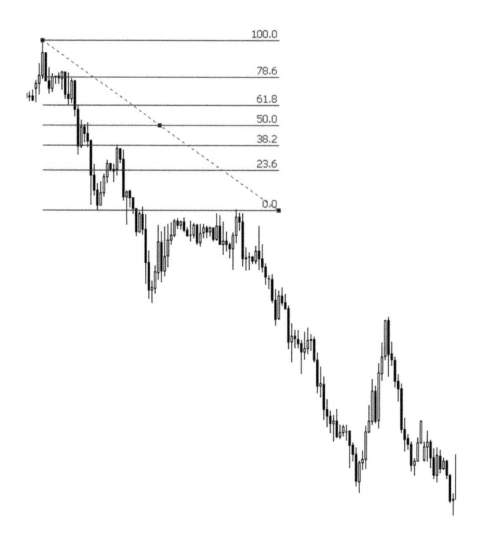

Notice how the price touched the 38.2 percent level before a strong sell-off happened. In this case, a shallow retracement was the signal for a prompt and strong bounce back to the original direction.

Identify an entry point

Once you know how to draw the retracement lines, you can open a trade at a better price.

But when should you enter a trade?

This is the biggest challenge after drawing the right retracements levels. You can find more specific guidance about entering a trade in Chapter 6 and Chapter 7. But before moving to those chapters, it is important that you understand some basic options you have when the price is approaching the retracement levels.

Let's look at the chart below.

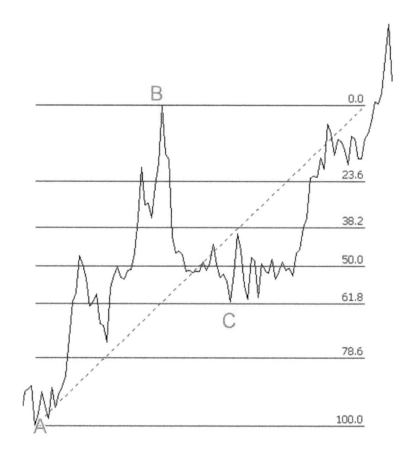

To make it simple, we're using a line chart. However, in your real trading, consider using a candlestick chart instead. A candlestick chart always provides more details than a line chart.

It is clear that an uptrend was dominant. After a swing move from A to B, there was a strong correction to C. In this scenario, we are waiting for a long position because the overall trend was bullish.

Now we have two options to open a position.

Option 1: Aggressive trading

In this case, you are willing to take a high risk in exchange for a possible big return. When the price (almost) reaches the 61.8 percent level, you place a long position. The 61.8 percent level is often considered a psychological level; hence, in many cases, the price may touch the level (or nearly touch if the counter side is very strong) and reverse.

Keep in mind that the 61.8 percent level is just for illustration purposes. In some cases, if your analysis points out that the price may retrace at other levels, you may choose to open the trade at those levels.

This is considered a dangerous type of trading. Remember that the price may not bounce to a new high. You are not aware whether the market will make a deeper correction or not. Applying this trading option may cause traders extreme anxiety.

One advantage of this method is that you **may** reap huge profits once the market goes according to your expectation.

Option 2: Conservative trading - using confirmation signals/triggers

In this method, you will execute your trade in conjunction with other confirmation signals and triggers that will better tilt the odds in your favor.

Still using the previous example, if you see that 61.8 percent is probably the retracement from which a bounce-back may occur, you should be prepared to take a long position.

However, unlike the first case, you wait for confirmation triggers.

In fact, Fibonacci patterns are best used in combination with candlestick patterns and indicators.

Waiting for confirmation triggers means waiting for the price to react at the Fibonacci levels. Among the best reaction for an entry would be a breakout, or a candlestick pattern (engulfing pattern, pin bar or double tops/bottoms, etc.).

When there is a confirmation signal, you go long. Remember that confirmation signals are not always 100 percent correct, and they do not ensure the profitability of the trades, either. However, when many indicators are pointing in the same direction, you can get a good idea of where the price is going.

Which one is better?

Some traders may be in favor of the first option to maximize potential profits. They argue that the second method may give them a worse entry price, which reduces their profits.

However, if you are patient enough, you are better at stacking the odds in your favor. Here is why:

-    As we discussed, Fibonacci does not work 100 percent of the time. If you doubt whether the market respects the Fibonacci level, you should wait for reliable confirmation from other tools and signals.

-    Although Fibonacci levels are often respected by the market, choosing an ideal entry level while ensuring good capital management can be difficult due to the enormous distance between levels. By having confirmation triggers, traders can easily place a more favorable stop-loss, setting a better risk/reward profile.

33

Each trader needs to practice multiple times before deciding which method works best for him/her. The method traders choose depends greatly on their trading skills, mental strength, trading styles, and more. To me, trading with at least one confirmation signal (other than Fibonacci) is what I choose most of the time.

In the following chapters, we'll describe **in detail** when and where to open your position by combining Fibonacci and different tools.

Place a stop-loss

Placing a stop-loss is a little tricky in trading with Fibonacci. Traders using Fibonacci in combination with candlestick patterns or price action may prefer a tighter stop-loss to enjoy a good risk/reward ratio. While we cannot deny its role in securing a long-term winning edge, trading this way may also be dangerous due to market volatility.

Now, let's refer to Fibonacci retracement levels to see some potential places for a stop-loss.

First, assume that you have a long position opened after a correction to point C in the chart below. Where should you place the stop-loss order?

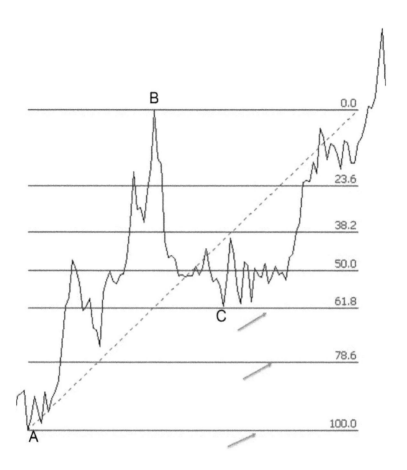

There are three options for you to choose from:

- The first option is just below the 61.8 percent level: It is the tightest stop-loss, offering the best risk/reward ratio. However, as I mentioned above, it could be affected by the market's volatility.
- The second option is just below the 78.6 percent level: It looks safer; however, during a highly volatile market, this stop-loss level may also be swept. The risk/reward ratio is not as good as in the first choice.

These are the two ways of setting stop-losses preferred by many traders. While it can be ideal in many cases, there are certain situations when they can see their stop-loss hit while their prior analysis still turns out to be right.

The third option is just below the 100 percent level. This method of stop-loss placement gives your trade more room to breathe among volatilities. A break below this level means that your trade is a loser. However, this method can lead to some unfavorable risk/reward ratios since you may have a wide stop that isn't proportional to your potential reward. Moreover, if you retain your position size while setting a wide stop-loss, you may incur a big loss, especially when you open your position at one of the early Fibonacci levels.

Which one is better?

To me, none of the three options is superior. The identification of stop-loss is highly dependent on each market situation, the formations of the candlestick, the willingness of risk-taking, and more. It would be best to use your knowledge of these elements to analyze each trading environment to pick a reliable stop-loss level.

In trading, stop-loss placement isn't a sure thing, and traders should not rely solely on Fibonacci lines as the basis for the stop-loss placement. Yet if you can combine many trading elements including Fibonacci tools, you are giving your trade more chance of success, starting with an appropriate entry and stop-loss point.

One last thing: If you ask me which option of the three methods I use the most in my trading, I would say the first and the second one.

CHAPTER 4: UNCOVERING THE ESSENCE OF FIBONACCI PROJECTION VALUES

In this chapter, you will learn about the Fibonacci projections and how you can use them to determine your exit point. This great tool provides the answer to the most important yet difficult task for a trader: where and when to stack profits.

The exiting technique

To make it clearer, the Fibonacci projections tools that we discuss in this Chapter include Fib extensions and Fib expansions. Many people refer to projections as expansions, which are different from extensions in the way they are plotted. This is just the way we call them and doesn't affect the way we trade. In any case, what you need to remember is that there are **two ways** of projecting price levels with Fibonacci to determine potential take-profit targets. The main difference between the two methods lies in the number of swing points we use to plot the levels. Specifically, with expansions, we use three swing points, while with extensions, we need only two. Don't worry because only two points are used to plot Fibonacci extension levels. A crucial thing to note is that both projection tools rely on Fibonacci magic ratios, then using one tool or the other should not cause much difference in the trade signals released.

We'll dive deeper into the plotting technique soon, but first, let's talk about the importance of Fibonacci projections.

Why are the Fibonacci projections so important?

One of the most important stages during the execution of a trade is identifying a profit-taking price. If you have been trading long enough, you may have experienced the bitter feeling of closing your trade at a loss or a break-even instead of a huge profit as expected. It can happen for many reasons, but from my experience, the main one has to do with a trader's failure to set a suitable and logical profit-taking target.

Remember that your ongoing profit will not be realized until the trade is closed. In other words, until you close the trade and take the profit, it is just a virtual profit. The market changes all the time. There can be some big news, the price may move against you, and in a couple of minutes, you may be counting how big your loss is.

This is the reason why closing trades is very important. To me, closing trades is far more important than opening them. Even a poorly opened trade can turn out to be profitable if you exit at the right moment. The question is when is the right time and where can you take profits?

The Fibonacci projection can help you to find the answers.

How to draw a Fibonacci price projection

- *With Fibonacci expansions*

We need three points to pinpoint a successful expansion.

These three points are determined during a trending market (an uptrend or a downtrend), namely A, B (the extreme points) and C (the retracement point).

Below are the necessary steps for drawing Fibonacci expansions:

- Identify the overall trend (up or down).
- Determine recent major swing highs and major swing lows.
- Connect the two extreme points A & B (from highest to lowest during a downtrend and from lowest to highest during an uptrend).
- Hold the cursor and drag from the major high (in an uptrend) and the major low (in a downtrend) to the retracement point ("C").

First, we draw a line from A to B as below.

Next, click on point B, then hold and move the cursor to point C, where the correction ends.

Now you have the potential levels the market may find. The three most popular are 61.8 percent, 100 percent, and 161.8 percent. According to the example below, an exit at the 161.8 percent level would help to catch most of the move.

The meaning of the targets

Remember that the expansion levels are calculated from point C:

- The 61.8 percent target is **0.618** times the distance between **A and B**
- The 100 percent target equals the distance between **A and B**
- The 161.8 percent target is **1.618** times the distance between **A and B**

That is why in the example above, the first target (61.8 percent) is just above point B. Before the trend resumed, a rather deep correction was made.

In another example, we draw the expansions within a downtrend. We need to make sure that the downtrend is strong before identifying a swing AB and a correction to C.

We start by connecting A and B.

Next, we click on B, dragging the cursor to C (where the correction ended).

The expansion levels are now drawn correctly. In this example, the price moved down strongly, and the 161.8 percent level would be a perfect target for a successful trade.

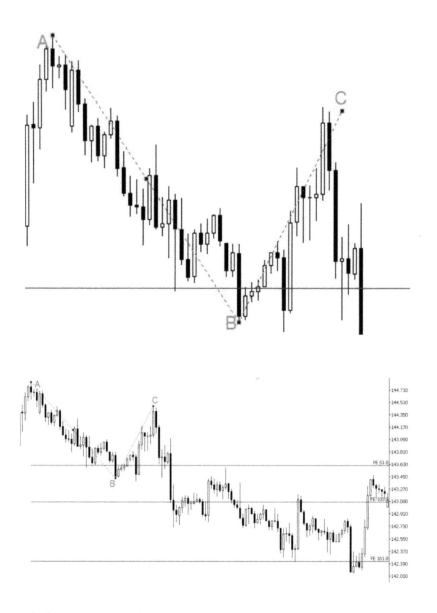

Now, let's move to another example to see how Fibonacci expansions can work well as both support and resistance.

The Gold Price Forecast chart below (XAU/USD) illustrates some Fibonacci expansion levels as well as the potential point D as a profit target. D is marked as the 100 percent advance or expansion from the retracement point C in the direction of the primary move. Note that CD is the same length as AB.

Looking at a bigger picture of the chart, we can see that there are levels that acted as strong support or resistance. Of prime importance is the 61.8 percent expansions level.

For example, a bearish trader opening a position soon after the swing high at C may look to the 61.8 percent expansion line as the first exit point, while the 100 percent expansion may be a secondary profit-taking target. Remember that the price often goes in a zig-zag shape. Once exhaustion is confirmed at the 100 percent expansion, the focus shifts toward the 61.8 percent level. The chart above illustrates the price rebounding off this mark before making a strong sell-off.

Looking a bit further, the 161.8 percent level worked the same when the price nearly touched it and reversed downward.

Now you can see how Fibonacci expansion levels (61.8 percent, 161.8 percent) can work well both as support and resistance levels. It is an illustration of the well-known theory that once a support level is broken, it can act as a reliable resistance level and vice versa.

- *With Fibonacci extensions*

Like Fibonacci retracements, Fibonacci extensions are drawn based on the two extremes of the swing only. Point C is not used for projections in this case.

Below are necessary steps for drawing Fibonacci extensions:

- Identify the overall trend (bullish or bearish).
- Determine recent major swing high and major swing low.
- Connect the two extreme points A & B (from highest to lowest during a downtrend, and from lowest to highest during an uptrend).

This distance between A and B is the standard distance. Accordingly, the extension levels will reflect the additional distance added to point B.

For example, the 138.2 percent extension level equals 1.382 times the distance between A and B, calculated from A.

44

You can see that point C (where the correction ends) is not used in this way of identifying extensions. Some people may suspect the reliability of the signal when C is not used. However, as stated earlier, this does not impose any bad impact on pinpointing support and resistance levels.

Personally, I prefer extensions to expansions when seeking price projections, mainly because I can combine extensions with retracements on the chart with only one action of dragging the cursor. In the last part of this book, I will show you a useful trick for combining the two tools on one chart so you can easily spot a bigger picture of market movements.

Some examples:

Have a look at the US dollar/ Japanese Yen (USD/JPY) chart below.

45

The market trend is upward, and you can easily identify point A and point B. In this case, we do not pay attention to exactly where the correction ends. Point C will be somewhere between A and B, but in order to calculate the extension, we need only A and B. This is what happens next:

The correction ended at the 61.8 percent retracement level and the price made a strong rally to the 200 percent extension level.

In another example of a downtrend market, we can also spot a correction back to the 61.8 percent retracement level. From that point, sellers showed up, and the price dropped to the 161.8 percent extension level after a few

more corrections.

Later in this book, I will present more examples of trades using both Fibonacci projections and retracements. For now, it is important that you understand the small difference between the Fibonacci extensions and expansions.

Expansions ⟶ 3 points (A, B, C) to identify the expansion levels

Extensions ⟶ 2 points (A, B) to identify the extension levels

As discussed above, my favorite tool is the Fibonacci extensions. You will see that in many examples in this book, I mainly use extensions. If you prefer the Fibonacci expansion, feel free to try it out and build your own trading strategies based on it.

Your expectation really matters

It is important to know that nothing is 100 percent certain in trading. You cannot know in advance where the price will stop. The projection levels should be treated as places where there is a possibility that the price will stop or even reverse.

Also, like retracements, extensions are not magnets to hold the price there.

In *Trading in the Zone,* author Mark Douglas says that Mr. Market does not care about each trader's expectation, analysis, or emotions. Sometimes the price stops for a while at the extensions and then continues if the trend is strong enough. In other cases, the move may reach or almost reach the extensions before bouncing back. That's why traders need to learn how to watch the price reaction at the extension levels closely (in conjunction with other tools) before making trading decisions.

CHAPTER 5: THE POWER OF FIBONACCI CONVERGENCE

A convergence occurs when you pull Fibonacci retracement lines for more than one swing. The interesting thing is that some levels from different Fibonacci settings occur in close proximity to each other on a price chart, making such levels/zones an even stronger indication of support/resistance.

The convergence can be very useful, but for new traders, it is not easy to use effectively right away. In this chapter, I will try to make it simple enough for all traders to apply in their trading.

Before trading with the Fibonacci convergence, you should feel comfortable with using the Fibonacci retracement and extension levels. You should be able to identify the price swing for setting Fibonacci grids. If you are not that experienced, do not worry! Over time, you will gain more experience in using retracement and extension.

Earlier, we discussed that in a trending market, the price often moves in a zigzag formation. I showed you how you can choose the swing to draw the Fibonacci retracements or extensions. Trends are built on many different swings. Interestingly, some different swings may produce similar Fibonacci retracement levels that become very solid support/resistance.

In the example below, the price moves up, creating swing highs and swing lows. There are some good swings to choose from to apply Fibonacci retracements.

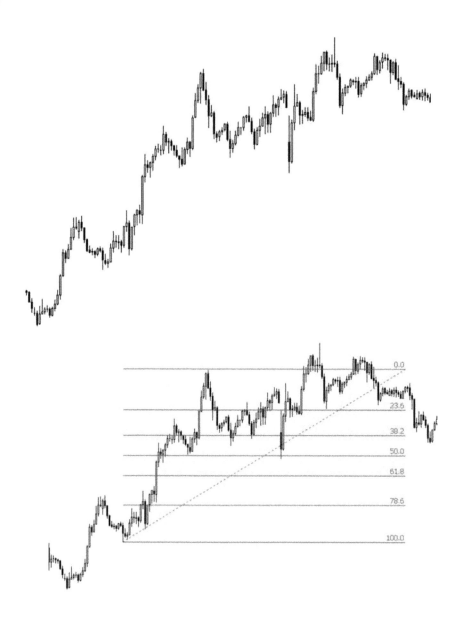

Below is one way to draw the retracements.

Also, we can use the swing high and swing low from a bigger range, where the price retraces back to the 38.2 percent levels.

When we put these two Fibonacci retracements together, we will see that some of them are at similar levels.

You will notice that the first convergence level was 61.8 percent level from the bigger range (BR) and 78.6 percent level from the smaller range (SR). Then, the second convergence was created between the 38.2 percent level (BR) and 50 percent level (SR). The price found a strong support level, and from that point, the uptrend continued.

Fibonacci confluence levels can be useful in a lot of trading applications, including finding optimal points of entry or identifying potential target levels for the close of the positions. They can also be used in conjunction with key horizontal price levels to help determine potential reversal areas. What's more, some traders may seek even stronger signals from the market by combining Fibonacci confluence levels with candlestick formations or other technical tools.

Moreover, it's necessary to understand that the heavier the confluence around a level is, the more likely it is for such a level to attract prices. For example, a Fibonacci confluence that is composed of three separate measurements would indicate a stronger support level than one that only consists of two Fibonacci measurements.

Last but not least, in terms of the Fibonacci tools themselves, a confluence can be created by just one Fibonacci tool or a combination of two or more tools. For example, a Fibonacci confluence can form using multiple Fibo retracements, or using Fibo retracements with Fibo extensions, or using two Fibo extensions. The more important the levels are, the stronger the confluence/cluster is.

CHAPTER 6: IDEAL TIME TO OPEN A POSITION

As you may remember, I mentioned earlier that the shallower the retracements are, the stronger the overall trend is.

A shallow pullback often appears around the 23.6 percent and 38.2 percent level, or anything which is not deeper than the 38.2 percent level.

Shallow pullbacks are typically seen within a **highly** trending market. When the market is moving strongly in one direction, it may not lose its steam for long before continuing its original trend. The breakout trading, in combination with Fibonacci tools, is a great choice during such an environment to better stack the odds in your favor while remaining a favorable risk/reward ratio.

There are two methods that you can consider using for opening a position.

Method 1: You take more risks

The principle of this method:

If we see a shallow retracement (i.e., not deeper than 38.2 percent), followed by a break through the previous swing high (within an uptrend) or swing low (within a downtrend), this would be the signal to open a position. The advantage of using this method is that it would reduce the possibilities of major losses while enabling potentially big gains.

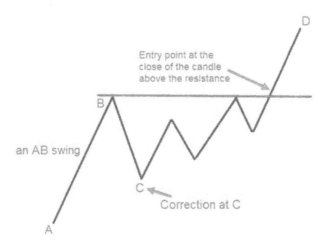

Entry point at the close of the candle above the resistance

B

an AB swing

C

Correction at C

A

D

In theory, it should look like the picture below.

Below are specific steps for a trade entry:

1. Identify the overall trend. You should be aware of what the overall trend is and in which direction you will be looking to enter a trade.
2. Determine the recent major swing high and major swing low to draw Fibonacci retracements and extensions.
3. After the price found the C retracement point, wait for the breakout above the swing high to go long in an uptrend (or below the swing low to go short in a downtrend). The entry point is the close of the price above the most recent swing high.
4. Wait for the price to hit a profit target based on Fibonacci extension levels (the D point).

Your exit point will be at one of the extension lines (more about closing positions in Chapter 8). Your goal is to catch most of the movement between the 0 percent level (point B) and the extension levels (i.e., 138.2 percent; 161.8 percent, 200 percent, etc.).

Examples

Let's take a look at the British pound to Japanese Yen chart below (GBP/JPY). It is clear from a long time frame that the overall trend is upward. After reaching B (the swing high during the uptrend), the market experienced a shallow correction to C (38.2 percent Fibonacci level). As I mentioned in Principle 3 above, we should wait for a breakout after point C is formed.

As you can see, after a while, there is a breakout above point B (the most recent high). The potential profit is huge in this trade (up to the 200 percent Fibonacci extension level).

Sometimes, due to high trading volumes, the market may explode through the most recent high/low very swiftly, forming a candlestick with a long body. As a result, the close of the candlestick may not be ideal for a trade entry due to its unfavorable risk/reward ratio. This is one problem that happens in a highly trending market. In those cases, just wait for another opportunity. Remember that the market is full of opportunities for you to catch.

The key to success in trading is patience and patience. On some trading days, you may have a couple of good or even very good setups and successful trades.

On other days, you might wait for a set up the whole day, but the market gives you nothing. It is advisable not to enter any trade during these times. Just wait for a good trade setup to appear before taking action.

The next example presents a four-hour WTI Oil chart. The overall trend was upward; hence, we looked for a buy entry. After a while, the AB swing presented, followed by a mild correction to C. Note that the price only retraced to the 23.6 percent Fibonacci level, indicating that the bulls were

strong enough to prevent the price from a deeper drop.

Notice how the price rocketed to the 161.8 percent extension line afterward, which was a strong resistance level and also the best exit point. Keep in mind that in a highly trending market like this, the price may not stop at the 161.8 percent level and reverse. You may choose to close part of your position at the 161.8 percent level and leave the remaining open to another potential target level. More on that in Chapter 8.

Let's see how this strategy can be used in a downtrend.

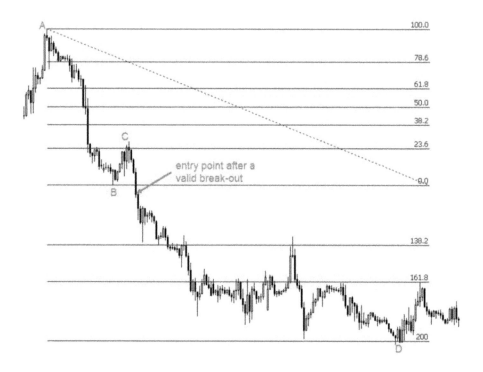

This is a daily chart of gold. The market was in a downtrend; hence, traders should look for a short entry. It is not difficult to find the AB swing. Still, the market created a shallow retracement at the 23.6 percent level. We wait for a breakdown below point B to enter a short position. The downward momentum was very strong, and it ended at the 200 percent extension line. Those who were using Fibonacci tools might have ended up with a huge profit.

Again, one advantage of using Fibonacci is that it can project a potential exit level **before the price's movement**, where both the risk-reward ratio and the profit are favorable. In this way, right from the beginning, Fibonacci helps traders have the best plan to exit a trade.

Stop-loss placement

Many traders may choose to place their stop "a few pips" below the broken level (a pip, or "percentage in point" is a small, incremental movement in price). However, by this method, they are not taking the mechanics of the market into consideration. As I mentioned, the market is full of volatilities; hence, such stop-loss orders may be triggered in many cases.

In fact, the price may revisit the prior areas a few times, but in the end, it still goes in the overall trend, and it is still a valid extension.

In this method, a wider stop-loss placement at just under the 23.6 percent level (in an uptrend) should be used. While it does not affect the risk/reward profile too much, it can reduce the adverse effect of the market's volatilities.

One concern may occur if the price fails to move in the underlying trend and comes back to the retracement levels. In this case, there may be something wrong with the overall trend strength (at least at that moment).

Suppose that instead of rising with the overall trend, the price moves back to the 23.6 percent retracement level. What will you do?

Some traders may move their stop-loss to the deeper levels (i.e., 38.2 percent or 61.8 percent), giving the market more room to breathe before they can enjoy their expected profits.

My recommendation is simple: When the price fails to move in the overall trend and comes back to the 23.6 percent level, just retain your stop-loss position. If your stop-loss is triggered, accept it.

Do not hope for the price to go in your expected direction. The market never knows what you want and how you plan your trade. The financial market is up and down all the time. When there is something that causes the price to go opposite to your expectation, accept it and look for another opportunity. Simple as that.

The stop-loss just below the 23.6 percent level is my suggestion. It is the level where I feel comfortable trading. If you feel the 14.6 percent level will make you comfortable with your trade, try it and analyze the overall results after a certain number of trades.

On the other hand, setting a stop much wider than the 23.6 percent level is not recommended. This way, your trade will not have a favorable risk/reward ratio.

Method 2: Wait for a retest

If you have some experience in trading, you will agree that nothing is 100 percent certain.

Let's take the uptrend as an example.

While a shallow retracement indicates that the underlying trend is strong, and there is a possibility that the market is likely to advance after a retracement, *it does not guarantee that such advance always happens.*

Sometimes, the market does witness a break through a support or resistance level, but then the price moves in a range for a period, causing some anxiety and confusion for breakout traders. Take a look at the example below.

The market failed to advance through a number of candlesticks later. If you took a trade right after the breakout candlestick, you might have experienced a loss.

The principle of this method

The idea behind this method is that you will not enter your trade until the price retests the broken support or resistance level. If you trade long enough, you'll know the double top and double bottom are popular, especially when you switch to a shorter time frame. Waiting for a retest before entering the trade would better enhance the probability of a successful trade.

In theory, it should look like the picture below.

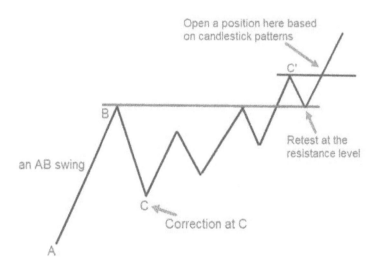

Below are specific steps for a trade entry:

1. Identify the overall trend. You should be aware of what the overall trend is and in which direction you will be looking to enter a trade.
2. Determine the recent major swing high and major swing low to draw Fibonacci retracements and extensions.
3. After the price found the C retracement point, wait for the breakout above the swing high, creating a new high at C.
4. From C, wait for the price to retest at the support and resistance level before continuing in the underlying trend.
5. The entry position is opened based on each candlestick pattern at the breakout level.
6. Wait for the price to hit a profit target based on Fibonacci extension levels.

Note: Candlestick patterns are a technical analysis tool that illustrates the movement in prices that are shown graphically on a candlestick chart. Some of the most popular candlestick patterns are pin bars, engulfing patterns, and marubozu.

I assume that you have some knowledge about candlestick patterns, so I am not describing them in detail. The main purpose of this book is to describe Fibonacci trading.

Take a look at the four-hour chart below where the market presents an AB swing and a correction to C.

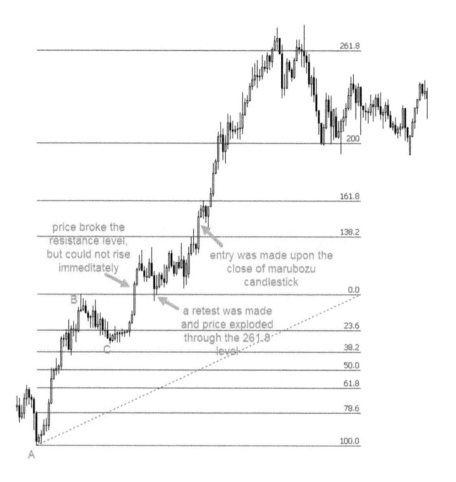

Below, we see the Fibonacci retracements were drawn, where the price broke above the B level. However, it could not rally until retesting the B level.

In this example, the retest is a perfect signal for the continuation of the original trend. The price never violated the support zone (note that the resistance level turns into a support level after it is broken) and from the retest, the price rocketed to the 261.8 percent extension level. With a stop-loss placed under the marubozu candlestick, you could obtain an ideal risk/reward profile of around 1:4.

Now you may argue that by taking more risk and opening the trade at the break of the B level, you may enjoy a bigger profit.

This may be true. However, remember that the most noticeable advantage of this method is to minimize the traps in the market, where the price may revisit the retracements a few times, causing your stop-loss to be hit. A retest at the B level (without breaking it to the downside) and an advance higher than the most recent high through a classic candlestick pattern would be a good signal that the price will probably go in the dominant trend.

Let's move to another example in a downtrend market. Below is the four-hour US dollar to Canadian dollar (USD/CAD) chart, where we can easily spot

A, B, and C in a Fibonacci retracement drawing.

Now let's see how the price reacted to the B-level after breaking it.

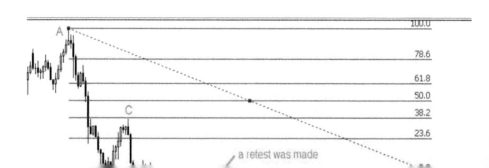

We can see that although the price made a shallow correction, it did not mean the price could easily continue in the original direction. Notice how difficult it was for the price to go down until it retested the most recent support, which then turned into a resistance level. Soon after the retest, a strong marubozu candlestick appeared, breaking the most recent low, signaling that a strong drop was about to come. You can see that although the price made some more efforts to increase, it could not go beyond the high of the marubozu candlestick, which is an ideal level for setting a stop-loss order.

Now let's see how far the price could go afterward:

The price plummeted to the 261.8 percent level with some small corrections along the way. You can see that although we did not join the trade earlier at the breakout point, we could still achieve a good risk-reward profile (around 1:3).

At this point, many conservative traders may be asking, "Hey Frank, what if the market doesn't retest the broken level (the B level)?" The answer is simple: As a conservative trader, I would pass on it and look for another opportunity.

There are not many guarantees I can make to a trader, whether you trade on stock, forex, or commodities. But there is one thing I can guarantee: **There will always be other opportunities tomorrow, so never force yourself to look for one today, which may negatively impact your account balance.**

Conclusion: Trading Fibonacci in conjunction with a retest and a breakout is among the best utilization of the powerful Fibonacci technique. From a technical perspective, if prices do retest the breakout level without breaking it, it is a signal that the breakout is valid. The market may develop a strong interest in the direction of the break.

Stop-loss placement

In this method, you can choose a stop-loss just below the candlestick patterns or just below the 23.6 percent level, depending on each market environment and your risk tolerance. To me, I use the former more often. However, if you are a more conservative trader, you may choose the 23.6

percent level.

How to avoid false breakouts

Traders may often be confused about a true breakout and a false breakout (commonly known as a fake-out). In fact, many seeming breakouts in the trading chart are actually fake-outs.

66

One trick to avoid false breakouts is to wait for the close of the candle to see where the closing price is. For example, when the close of the candle is on the other side of the resistance/support line and the shadow of the candle is small compared to the body, it may be considered a breakout.

The GBP/JPY chart below can illustrate this trick. We have one support level at 149.138. As you can see, the first and second attempts were both false breakouts because the close of those candles were above the support level. Finally, there was another attempt, but unlike the previous ones, that candlestick successfully poked through the support line. It was the signal to enter a selling trade.

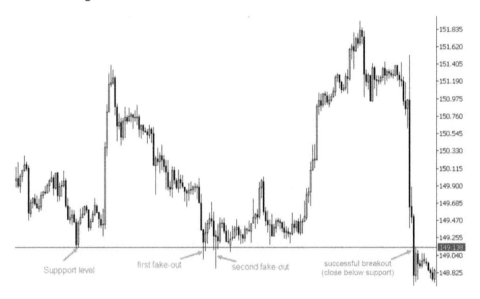

Again, please note that the market is full of volatilities, and this confirmation signal does not work well all the time. However, to me, it turns out to be correct in many cases.

Below are some notes on trading based on strategies presented in this chapter:

1. Lines or zones?

The price may not make it exactly back to the breakout level. This is why you should consider marking a support or resistance zone instead of a line in some cases. In the above examples as well as throughout this book, I am using a line for better visualization and understanding.

2. Pending orders

From my experience, taking a trade based on the retest of a breakout point should not be executed by using a pending order. It may put the trade in danger where you don't gather enough confirmation signals of market strength.

You cannot know in advance whether the support or resistance level is going to hold or not before the price "retests" it. Hence, if you place a pending order and the price pushed through it instead of bouncing back, your stop-loss is highly likely to be swept.

3. Other effective methods

In this chapter, I have shown you the two methods that I often use in trading a shallow retracement.

However, it does not mean that you can only use these strategies to trade when the price makes a mild correction. In fact, there are many ways to open a position relating to each type of market formation.

In the next chapter, I will share with you some effective strategies which can be applied in any type of Fibonacci retracement.

Remember these strategies do not only apply to deep and mid-sized pullbacks, but can be used during a shallow correction as well. This is why in some examples presented below, you will see the price retrace to shallow levels like the 38.2 percent line.

In general, you will take more risks using the strategies presented in this chapter, but there is logic behind this. You can look for an earlier entry instead of waiting for the price to break through the previous swing low or swing high. As a result, your profits are potentially higher.

The principle

With this method, traders will join a trade earlier, somewhere between the support level (drawn from point C—the correction point) and the resistance level (drawn from point B—the swing high).

The above strategy applies to an uptrend. Regarding the downtrend, the principle is similar, but in the opposite direction.

The picture below illustrates the principle.

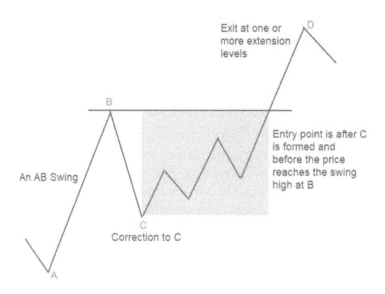

Exit at one or more extension levels

An AB Swing

Entry point is after C is formed and before the price reaches the swing high at B

Correction to C

Here are the necessary steps for opening a position:

1. Identify the underlying trend. You should be aware of what the underlying trend is and in which direction you will be looking to enter a trade.
2. Determine the recent major swing high and major swing low to draw Fibonacci retracements and extensions.
3. Wait for the end of the correction to point C.
4. After the price has found a correction point, continue to wait for another **confirmation signal** to open a position.
5. Close the trade at one or more extension levels.

You can see that a few steps are similar to the previous methods. However, the key point lies in the most important part of the method.

I mentioned in Chapter 3 how trading Fibonacci in conjunction with other tools can provide reliable signals. This is what many savvy Fibonacci traders often do because the more confirmation signals your trade has, the higher probability of success your trade can achieve.

Let's go back to the core of the strategy. Assume we are in an uptrend, and point C has been determined in the chart as the end of the retracement.

70

Now we are prepared for a long entry. The question is: When should we open the position?

We should not take a risk by opening a position right at the retracement level.

If you notice on the chart, when the market accepts the retracement and goes back in the underlying direction, there is often at least **a signal somewhere between point C and point B, and this is what we look for.**

You may be wondering what kind of signal we are looking for.

The answer is that it varies. It may be a signal in the form of a candlestick pattern, support/resistance, or a trend line, etc. The more you investigate and practice, the better you will be at identifying which signal works best in each situation. In this chapter, I will introduce the most popular confirmation signals in trading with Fibonacci.

Let's take a look at the chart below.

In this case, the signal is a break above the trend line. As you can see, after making a 50 percent correction at C, the price moved in a range before breaking above the trend line, paving the way for a clear uptrend.

THE CONFIRMATION SIGNALS

Here are some of the best confirmation signals that you can consider looking for when choosing an entry price between point B and point C.

Confirmation 1: A trend line

Among the best ways of using Fibonacci retracements to identify an entry price is through combining it with trend lines.

In an uptrend or a downtrend, it can be easy for traders to draw the trend lines. A trend line is a typical example of a trending market. Combining the trend line with Fibonacci retracement levels could bring you a winning trading strategy.

After determining the overall trend in the market, you can draw the trend

line by connecting swing lows or swing highs.

Let's assume you are waiting for a retest on this trend line. Meanwhile, you can also draw the Fibonacci retracement levels from a major swing low to a major swing high.

In the above example, we can see how prices bounced off the trendline which also coincided with the 38.2 percent level, providing a nice confluence support zone. Combine a trend line with retracement levels, and you have a high probability, low-risk trade setup in place.

Remember that this combination does not work 100 percent of the time, but it proves to be a great combination. Strong trend lines are often associated with psychological effects where sellers tend to lock in profits. Sellers closing their trades means buyers are establishing their long positions and the price bounces back.

Confirmation 2: Support/resistance levels

One of the most effective methods to use the Fibonacci retracement tool is to combine it with support or resistance levels. Many experienced traders agree that once a resistance level is breached, it tends to act as a future support level. Similarly, once a support level is broken, it may act as a future resistance level. Combining Fibonacci retracements with support and resistance levels may help to boost your trading performance.

Remember that the Fibonacci levels themselves are considered support and resistance. If you combine them with other price areas that already form support and resistance, then the chances of the price bouncing back from those areas are even higher.

Below is a four-hour chart of gold.

You decide that the market is trending up, and you want to go long on the commodity.

The question is: When and where should you open your position?

The first step in finding a reliable entry price is by using Fibonacci retracements to point out potential correction levels after the price reaches the swing high at B.

Now that we have some Fibonacci retracement levels on the chart, the next step is to decide which level to choose.

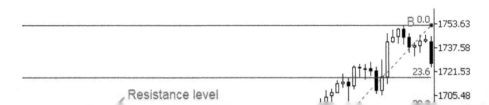

In this case, support and resistance can help you.

Looking back a bit, and we can see a good resistance level in the past. It coincided with the **38.2 percent** Fibonacci level.

Now that it was broken, it could turn into a reliable support level, which is a good place for a long entry. Let's see what happened next in the picture below:

If you did place an order around the 38.2 percent Fibonacci level, you might have enjoyed your profits.

You can apply the same method during a downtrend as well. The point is that you should find some price levels that seemed to generate interest in the past. The support/resistance level itself is the area that attracts most traders' attention when the price starts to approach it. Most traders are in a position for a long/short at a support/resistance level. Hence, when combining Fibonacci with these levels, there is a high probability that the price will bounce from these confluence levels/areas.

Confirmation 3: Candlestick patterns

You have learned that each Fibonacci retracement line can work as a support or resistance level. Moreover, if the price reverses near a strong support and resistance level, in most cases, you will find a reversal candlestick pattern. It is the reason why combining Fibonacci with candlestick patterns may help to take your trading result to the next level.

Below is a four-hour chart of British pound/Japanese yen (GBP/JPY).

In the chart above, we can see the market rallied from the swing low at A to the swing high at B, indicating the strength of the underlying uptrend. Trading at a retracement of any strong move is always advisable to traders. Now let's plot the Fibonacci levels on the chart:

77

Notice the long bullish candle, which touched the 50 percent Fibonacci retracement level before engulfing the previous bearish candlestick. It is a typical example of both a marubozu candlestick and an engulfing candlestick. These are two of the best candlestick confirmation signals which notify that the bullish side was gaining strength back again and was ready to push the price higher very soon. You should be prepared to go long then, with a stop-loss below the long bullish candlestick.

Below is what happened next.

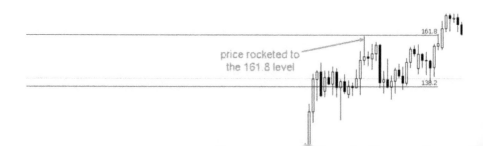

The price went up and easily found the first resistance at an ideal level of 161.8 percent Fibonacci extension. You can see how powerful candlestick patterns are when combined with Fibonacci retracements and extensions and help identify the entry, stop-loss, and profit-taking levels.

Confirmation 4: Moving averages

Another great confirmation signal is moving averages. You probably know that some popular averages work well as support and resistance.

Among the most commonly used moving averages are 10, 20, 50, 100, and 200 periods long.

Some traders may argue that there are other important moving averages. In my opinion, this is something you should decide based on your trading style. From the above set of averages, the most important are the longest ones: 50, 100, and 200. If you can connect at least one of these levels with the Fibonacci retracement to seek a confluence in trading, you stand a good chance of picking a good entry point.

Below is a four-hour chart of the S&P500. You can see that the price was above the 50 SMA. The Fibonacci retracement levels are plotted from a bigger swing of the market. Notice how the retracement at C coincided with the 50 percent Fibonacci level. This is obviously a reliable level to re-join the bearish movement.

From another perspective, since the moving average is considered a support/resistance level, a move to break through it means a support/resistance level has been broken, enabling an entry.

One of the signals I often pay attention to is the candlestick's close above (or below in the downtrend) the 50 SMA. In many cases, when the price closes above that level, it is a signal that the momentum is changing. As can be seen below, after the correction to the 50 percent level, I would wait for a trade after the candlestick closes below the 50 SMA.

The moving averages crossover

Sometimes, a crossover between two moving averages may confirm that the correction is over and the underlying trend is ready to continue.

You can choose your preferred set of moving averages on trading with Fibonacci. From my experience, there is no set of moving average that is 100 percent superior to the others. Some prefer faster MAs, while others like slower averages.

In the example below, there are two simple moving averages: 10 SMA and 20 SMA. The overall trend was bearish. After the correction up to the 61.8

80

percent level, the price fell sharply. When the 10 SMA crossed below the 20 SMA, you received a good confirmation signal to place a sell entry.

Again, the 10 SMA and 20 SMA are only shown as examples here. You may prefer another set of moving averages. It's okay. Keep using them as long as you are benefitting from them.

Some of you may wonder why I don't simply give you one standard set of MAs to follow.

As you may already know, some traders often stick to the four-hour chart. In this time frame, some MAs work better than others. Other traders may prefer a five-minute chart, where other MAs may produce better signals.

Choosing a favorite set of SMA entails practicing, with trials and errors. It is not a quick decision. It needs patience and enthusiasm.

Stop-loss placement

Stop-loss should not be thought of as rigid levels in these trading strategies. In particular:

- **Rethinking Stop-Loss: A Fluid Approach in Your Trading Arsenal**

- If the correction is from the 50 percent to the 61.8 percent level, a stop-loss below the 78.6 percent retracement level or below the most recent low may be placed, depending on the risk tolerance of each trader. The latter may save you from high volatilities in the market but offers a less favorable risk/reward profile than the former.

-    If C ends at the 78.6 percent retracement level, a stop-loss below the 100 percent level can be a good idea. A break down below the prior swing low means your analysis is invalidated and you should exit your position. Moreover, by placing our stops below the prior trough, we can ensure an advantageous risk-reward (R/R) profile. For example, a long entry around the 78.6 percent Fibonacci level, with the stop placed just below the 100 level, would provide a 1:3 R/R ratio for a short move back into the previous peak (0 percent).

  • On the other hand, if you are a more flexible trader, you may prefer to set a stop-loss just below the confirmation signal (i.e., just below the low shadow of a candlestick in a breakout) in an uptrend or just above that signal in a downtrend. It is easier for your stop-loss to be triggered, but your R/R profile is now much better than the two methods above.

Also, please note that these are only proposing where you can place your stop-loss, based on my own experience. To me, they work in many cases, but I cannot guarantee that they will work on every single trade of yours.

83

Moreover, there can be other good ways of stop-loss placement that you can adopt from your own trading experience.

You should practice on real charts multiple times and choose the one that works best for you. For each trader, their preferred stop-loss may vary over time; hence, practice is the key. In case you are not confident in setting your stop-loss, you can refer to the levels suggested above.

Of the three above levels, determining your profit target is by far the most difficult because it's a combination of both science and art. In fact, where you place your profit level can have a considerable impact on your trading profitability.

The problem with most traders is that they concentrate too much on finding the best entry price.

However, the "best price" has more to do with where you exit your trade.

For example, Trader A might go long on GBP/USD at 1.4100 and get out at 1.4120 for 20 pips profit. Meanwhile, Trader B might go long at 1.4110 but exit at 1.4150 for 40 pips profit. Hence, even though Trader A opened the position at a "better" price, Trader B ended up with a bigger profit.

By saying this, I don't mean that where you open your trade and where you set your stop-loss order is not important. What I mean is placing a suitable profit-taking level is even more important than choosing an entry and a stop-loss level.

Luckily, Fibonacci extensions can help you do this.

Principle: No fixed rules

Trading is all about probability; hence, we should not use a fixed level of profit-taking. The art of defining a profit target depends on each market environment as well as the trader's trading style, which I will discuss later in this chapter. But first, let me give you a little trick that you can apply in many cases.

THE THREE-PART METHOD

The idea behind this method is that it saves you from losing what should have been your profits. Also, it saves you from greed—one of the biggest enemies to all traders in the financial markets. Using this trick helps you protect your trading capital.

How to apply the method

First, you don't close all of your positions at any price level. Instead, you do it step-by-step, combined with raising the stop-loss level to enjoy profits.

Accordingly, the first target should be the 127 percent level or 138 percent level, depending on where you open the trade. After that, if the price still goes in your expected direction, continue to close the second part at the 161.8 percent level or 200 percent level. Regarding the final third of the position, you may base on another support/resistance, candlestick patterns, or some other market signals to stack your profit.

One thing to note on using this trick is that the stop-loss needs to be raised to the entry point after the first part of the position is closed.

Let's take an example to make it clearer.

In the example below, the correction ends at the 50 percent retracement level. Notice how the market formed a perfect pin bar at this level, with its closing price right above the mid-point level. An entry position could be placed at the close of this candlestick. When the trade was profitable, the first part was closed at the 127 percent extension level. Because the price continued to rise, the second part is closed at the 161.8 percent level. You might then feel comfortable looking for another exit signal to close the third part of the trade.

In the example above, the market was highly trending. However, if you doubt the probability of a continued strong move in the overall direction, consider closing the second part at the 138 percent extension. Look at how the market made a mild correction when the price reached the 138.2 percent extension above.

Sometimes, the first target is hit, but the price won't reach the next Fibonacci level.

In the example below, a downtrend was present. The correction was deep, up to the 61.8 percent retracement level. The entry point was at the

candlestick's close below the 50 MA.

It was going nicely down to the 127 percent extension level, where the first part of the position closed. Suddenly, buyers showed up. The price reversed and started to rise. There were still two parts of the position open, but the stop-loss had been moved to the entry point. It is crucial to do that for management purposes.

The rise continued. Eventually, we got stopped out, but still, we closed the trade with a profit.

This is how it works. At times, you get lucky: The trend is strong, and you can close all three parts at higher levels. On other occasions, you will be stopped out with a loss, or a profit from the close at the first extension level.

If this principle is too complicated for you, start by dividing your position into two parts and enjoy the benefits from it. To me, **capital preservation should be the number one priority in trading.**

HOW TO TAKE PROFITS:

Now let's come to the most important part of this chapter: where to set the profit-taking order for your trade.

As I mentioned, taking profits should be based on each market environment as well as the trader's trading styles. Let's move to some scenarios below:

1. A strong trend with a shallow retracement

The strength of the ongoing trend may help to determine the distance of the move. A short retracement followed by a swift bounce back into its original direction may indicate that the trend is strong. In this case, a target at least at the 161.8 percent level or the next major support/ resistance level should be considered. Take a look at the four-hour chart of Gold below:

Price rose to the
161.8 level promptly

161.8

138.2

127

50 SMA

price bounced
from the 50 SMA

Notice how the 50 SMA acted as perfect support at the 38.2 percent level. At this shallow retracement line, a long bullish candlestick pattern formed, strongly supported by the 50 SMA. This was a great confluence (Fibonacci retracement, candlestick pattern, and 50 SMA) to place a long entry. It did not take long for the price to reach the 161.8 percent level and the 200 percent level.

Sometimes, if certain volatilities occur during the resumption of the trend, you may consider applying the three-part method discussed above. This method may help to save you from the unexpected reverse of the price. The act of dividing your profit-taking into three stages would better secure the success of the trade.

In this case, the last close should be based on support/resistance or a form of reversal candlestick pattern. Still from the above example, when looking at the past, we would see a resistance level present at the 200 percent extension line. As such, the next potential profit target should be the 200 percent level.

2. The market creates a mid-sized/deep retracement

A deep retracement at the 78.6 percent level may indicate that the underlying trend lacks strength and momentum. In this case, choosing a 138.2 percent level may be a more suitable decision.

Regarding a correction to the 61.8 percent, while it is considered a deep retracement, it is also considered the golden ratio in trading. Hence, you should pay more attention to that level. Profit-taking price may be higher, at the 161.8 percent line, or the next major support/resistance level. However, since the momentum may not be as strong as in the case of a shallow retracement, the three-part method should be considered in this scenario.

Similarly, regarding the 50 percent correction, an exit of around the 161.8 percent line, in conjunction with the three-part method may be a good choice in many cases.

If you are a more conservative trader, you may want to choose an exit around the 138.2 percent level. However, remember that sometimes, the market may explode through this level.

Take a look at the example below.

91

The market was in a downtrend, correcting at the 61.8 percent level. Right after touching this level, an engulfing pattern appeared, pulling the price down to the 127 percent level, where the first part of the position should be closed. Notice how the market reacted strongly at this level but could not sweep the stop-loss (which had been raised to the entry price).

Then the market continued its bearish momentum, going down to the 161.8 percent level. Those who used the three-part method would have enjoyed the profit of the trade.

3.   Your risk appetite really matters

Above all, the degree of your risk tolerance may affect your trading decision.

If you are an aggressive trader who is willing to take risks, you might choose a profit level around the 161.8 percent line or higher, whereas a conservative trader may opt for the 138.2 percent level or even the 127 percent level. Moreover, a three-part method may be adopted by them most of the time because they may put trading capital much higher than profitability in their priority order.

Let's come back to the example above.

We can see that the market made a deep pullback. A conservative trader may not be so confident in a strong bearish move afterward. They may choose to close the whole profit at the 127 percent level or 138.2 percent level. Notice how the price reacted strongly after touching the 127 percent level.

On the other hand, an aggressive trader may be more optimistic. They understand the 61.8 percent is a golden ratio, and a correction at this level may be the start of a strong resumption afterward. Instead of choosing 127 percent or 138.2 percent as the profit target, they may be in favor of the three-part method. The first and second close should be made at 127 percent and 161.8 percent, and the last third could be left open to another major support level.

Sometimes, there is no "right" or "wrong" in choosing the profit-taking price. It is how you feel in case of a win or a loss that helps you decide which level to choose for profit-taking.

Note: Similar to the entry price, keep in mind that the price may almost reach your desired profit level and suddenly reverse.

93

This can result from the fact that many other traders also keep their eyes on that level. When the price is approaching the level, many of them may close their trades just before you do, causing an unexpected reversal.

Closing your trade just a few pips below/above the exact price level is highly recommended. By doing this, you increase your chances of closing your trade while your profit is not considerably affected.

With that said, on certain occasions, the price may move beyond the extension level. As I mentioned above, it is part of trading, and you should accept it. The most important thing is to have a plan that can give you reliable exit points. Over time, you will realize your progress by consistently applying what you should do and avoiding what you should not do. Trading is all about long-term results.

Conclusion

While many traders find it difficult to be profitable in the financial markets, there are some who are. These traders constantly talk about "what wave we are in." Elliott waves are a *predictive tool* that can be beneficial to many traders. Like Fibonacci, Elliott waves give you an idea of where the markets may go.

Elliott Wave helps us identify the dominant trend and the countertrend. Within the former, the moves in the direction of the trend are known as the impulse moves while those in the countertrend are referred to as corrective moves.

A typical dominant trend tends to unfold in five waves: (1) impulse, (2) corrective, (3) impulse, (4) corrective, and (5) impulse.

Let's take a look at the five waves in the following uptrend.

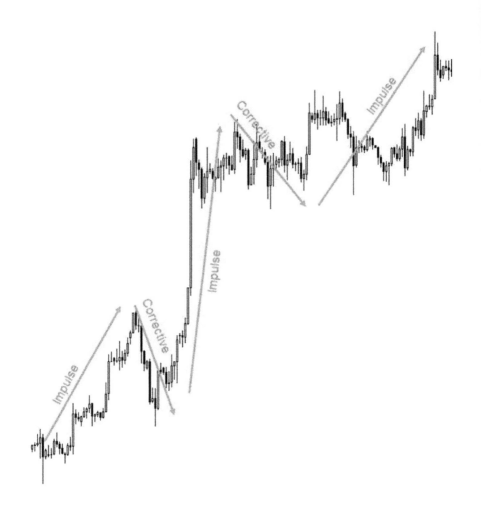

An Examination of the Ascending Five-Wave Cycle

Regarding the countertrend, it often includes three waves, normally known as A, B, and C. The picture below illustrates both the dominant trend and countertrend.

Here are some rules for a standard Elliott Wave cycle.

Dominant trend (the motive phase):

- ## The Mainstream Course: Understanding the Motive Phase

- Wave 3 is never the shortest among the five waves. In many cases, Wave 3 is the longest.

- Wave 4 cannot enter the territory of Wave 1.

- There is often an extended wave among the three impulse waves.

Countertrend (the corrective phase):

1. ## The Counter-Movement: The Corrective Segment
2. Wave C exceeds the end of Wave A.

HOW TO COMBINE FIBONACCI TOOLS WITH ELLIOTT WAVES IN TRADING

This is where Fibonacci tools get exciting. As you already know, Fibonacci extensions help us with predictive price targets while Fibonacci retracements suggest possible price stops after a strong move. When we combine Fibonacci tools with Elliott waves, they may allow us to enjoy continual profits in trading.

Below, I will analyze how you can apply Fibonacci techniques in each of the waves in the dominant trend.

- **Wave 1:**

Usually, there are no projection points within this wave, simply because this is your starting point and there is not a retracement area yet.

- **Waves 2 & 4:**

If you have some experience in trading, Wave 2 tends to be a deep retracement in comparison with wave 1: i.e., 50 percent, 61.8 percent, and 78.6 percent. Sometimes, it may just correct at 38.2 percent.

Meanwhile, Wave 4 tends to be a shallow retracement in comparison to Wave 3. Understandably, Wave 3 is normally the longest; hence, Wave 4 may not be a deep retracement. Otherwise, it can violate the territory of Wave 1. The pullback of Wave 4 often ranges from 23.6 percent to 50 percent. Sometimes, it may go back to 61.8 percent, but chances are small.

This leads to a strategy on trading pullbacks by finding a confluence between Fibonacci and Elliott waves. A deep retracement of Wave 2 to around 50 percent, 61.8 percent, or 78.6 percent level may pave the way for a potential bullish move afterward. Let's look at the picture below.

As can be seen, Wave 2 is quite deep (at around 78.6 percent of Wave 1). Opening the trade at the close of the engulfing pattern right at the retracement level would have let you ride a very long wave (Wave 3 + Wave 5). Notice Wave 4 was only a shallow correction after Wave 3 completed. Moreover, the picture illustrates one more important correlation between the two corrective waves: If one of them (Wave 2) is simple, the other (Wave 4) tends to be complex, and vice versa. Also, in this case, Wave 5 is the extended wave. The market was totally dominated by the bears.

- **Wave 3:**

Remember there is often at least one extended wave among the three impulse waves. Everyone wants to ride the extended wave, as it is the wave that has two characteristics every trader craves: huge and quick profits.

In the above example, Wave 5 is the extended one. However, statistics show that in most cases, Wave 3 is the extended one. As you already know, this wave cannot be the shortest among the three impulse ones.

Now, assuming you believe an extended wave in a five-wave string is forming, there are a couple things to do to identify a possible target of the price's movement. Luckily, Fibonacci expansions can help.

In Chapter 3, we learned how to draw Fibonacci expansions using three points: A, B, and C. A valid extended wave must be at least 161.8 percent of the distance between point A and point B. It means that the target should at least be the 161.8 percent expansion level.

Take a look at the illustration below:

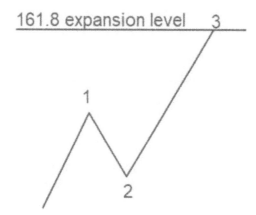

Keep in mind that extended waves are often explosive moves, and this helps to explain why traders often have a strong interest in these waves. Also, the 161.8 percent extension level is actually the minimum level to be considered an extended wave. In fact, the extensions may go all the way to the 261.8 percent or 461.8 percent level. This is how important it is to ride the wave with Fibonacci and Elliott waves.

Take a look at the daily chart of New Zealand and US dollar (NZD/USD) below.

Wave 5

Wave 3

Close the trade at 261.8% Fib
level with a risk/reward profile
at 1:7

261.8

Wave 4

200

161.8

138.2

127

Wave 1

0.0

23.6

38.2

50.0

61.8

Wave 2

enter the trade at the
close of the long
bullish marubozu

78.6

100.0

As you can see, Wave 2 was once again a deep retracement, with the close of the candle just at the 61.8 percent level. From that point, the price rocketed without any considerable counter move. The end of Wave 3 was above the 261.8 percent level, and those joining the wave would have been profitable. In this case, with a stop-loss placed below the 61.8 percent level and the profit-taking target at the 261.8 percent level, you may achieve a wonderful risk/reward ratio of 1:7.

- **Wave 5:**

This wave is not expected to go very far, especially when Wave 3 is extended. Yet you can still make use of trading Wave 5 based on the performance of Wave 4.

As mentioned above, Wave 4 is often a shallow retracement, with an expected correction not deeper than the 50 percent level. A retracement from 61.8 percent to 78.6 percent is less likely. Keep in mind that if Wave 2 is a deep retracement, the chances of Wave 4 being a shallow retracement are even higher (the rule of alternation in the Elliott Wave cycle).

As such, a position opened around the 23.6 percent level or 38.2 percent level can be a good way to trade Wave 5. The next important question relates to when and where to put profit-taking levels.

One trick to calculate the potential target is by comparing the length of Wave 5 to the distance from the start of Wave 1 to the end of Wave 3. One target to aim for is the 38.2 percent distance from Wave 1 to Wave 3. It may go to 61.8 percent of the distance, though it's less likely.

Let's take a look at the illustration image below for a better understanding.

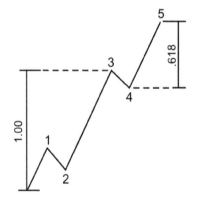
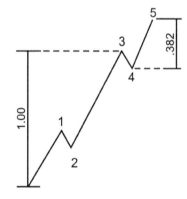

If you still remember the use of Fibonacci expansions, you can easily measure the potential target of Wave 5, with A at the beginning of Wave 1, B at the end of Wave 3, and C at the end of Wave 4.

Now, let's move to a real example to see how this can be applied to determine a potential target for Wave 5.

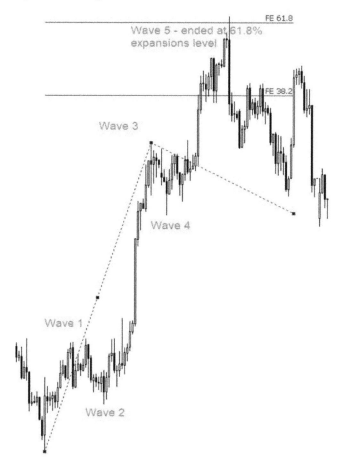

The daily EUR/USD chart above witnessed an extended Wave 3 before a mild corrective Wave 4 formed. After a few volatilities within the fourth wave, the market continued its bullish trend in Wave 5, ending at the 61.8 Fibonacci expansion. Notice the expansions are drawn from the beginning of Wave 1 to the end of Wave 3, then drag to the end of Wave 4.

Keep in mind that Wave 3 was extended, so it was not very likely for Wave 5 to go very far. A target from 38.2 percent to 61.8 percent expansion level is more appropriate in this case.

With that in mind, the length of Wave 5 can be much longer if it is the extended wave (take a look at the example early in this chapter). If Wave 3 cannot reach or nearly reach the 161.8 percent level, chances are that Wave 5 will be a candidate for the extension. In that case, you should be prepared for a further move. The three-part method discussed in Chapter 8 should be used in that scenario.

In general, trading Wave 5 can be a good idea if the market is in a strong trend, and you want to add more positions to your trading.

In short, Elliot counts in conjunction with Fibonacci may produce extremely reliable results. While traders may pay most of their attention to Wave 3, understanding waves based on Fibonacci retracements may give them the best option on entering a trade. Wave 5 may be an ideal choice for adding a position to your trading, based on a pre-defined end of Wave 4. Fibonacci expansions play a strong role in pinpointing potential targets for both Wave 3 and Wave 5.

CHAPTER 10: SECRETS OF BETTER TRADE MANAGEMENT

The market provides a number of trading opportunities every day. Sometimes, you may be so excited about a trading setup that you increase your trading size by two or three times, or even more. At other times, you may be so angry and depressed about a loss that you open many successive positions even though the signals are not clear enough to do so under your original set of rules.

While emotions can affect your ability to make smart decisions, it is impossible to switch them off completely. This is why you need to learn about how to manage your emotions so your trading aligns with your intended rules and guidelines.

Below are some effective ways to keep your trading on track.

1. Stop-losses and the two percent rule

Some traders never set stop-losses. They are afraid that when their stop-loss is hit, they will miss a good opportunity. They are afraid of missing potential profits. But remember, they are also the ones who are often praying for the price to come back in their expected direction, only to see their loss become bigger and bigger.

As a trader, you should always set a stop-loss for your trades.

Along with setting a stop-loss, another important consideration is how much you risk for each trade. You have probably heard about the 2% rule. The main idea is that you should not risk more than 2% of your current trading capital in each trade. For example, if your trading account balance is $10,000, you should not risk more than $200.

If you want to risk more, you need to increase your trading capital. While this guidance may seem difficult to follow, it is what you **should do.** Trading should be seen as a long-term journey instead of overnight prosperity.

Good capital management helps you succeed on that journey. As you may have heard, the number one rule in trading is to preserve your capital. The number two rule is to "never forget rule number one."

What to do if your account is not big enough

If your account is not big enough, simply execute your trades using smaller amounts. By doing this, you will be able to adhere to the 2% risk principle.

You may argue that by using smaller amounts, it is hard to generate enough profits. You may think trading this way is a little bit boring.

Remember that trading is a long-term endeavor, which requires a lot of practice and patience. While starting small may seem dull, by doing so you will gain invaluable experience and techniques, which will lead to positive results and bigger and bigger profits. After all, isn't that the reason you started trading?

Any better ways to enjoy the trades?

As I mentioned, it is not easy to follow the rules all the time. In fact, some traders violate the rule on their very first trades.

If you want to risk more than 2% of your account, believing that you are ready for it, then take this advice: Divide your trading capital into two separate accounts, with 80% of your money in one and 20% in the second.

You are going to trade using both accounts, but with different approaches.

With the bigger one, you must stick to the 2% rule, because this is where most of your money is and you must protect it at all costs.

The second account is where you can trade with a bigger risk percentage per trade. If you can make good trading decisions, both of your accounts will grow. With the higher risks taken in the second account, you will have bigger profits in total.

If, however, your trading decisions seem to be wrong, don't worry - you only took the greater risks with a smaller percentage of your capital, so the loss will not be so psychologically painful. While you may lose quite a bit of money from the smaller account, most of your cash will be preserved and under control in the bigger account.

By dividing your account into two separate ones, you will have a deeper understanding of whether you are ready to trade with bigger positions. Sometimes, traders are in over their heads without realizing it. They are not aware of the dangers of trading in big position sizes. By trading more conservatively with the two accounts for a limited initial period, they can realize a deeper trading zone.

2. Raising the stop-loss order

I mentioned raising stop-losses in previous chapters. Raising the stop-loss is one of the best ways to managing your trades effectively.

In previous chapters, I recommend you move the stop-loss order when your trade is profitable. However, you needn't do this immediately. You can do this step-by-step based on market conditions.

Let's say, for example, you open a position and set the stop-loss 10 points below the entry point. The price is going up and is about to break through the most recent resistance level. You then choose to raise the stop-loss to be only 5 points below the entry point. Afterward, the price continues to advance higher and the first target (i.e., the 127% level) is hit. In this situation, you should close one-third of your position and raise the stop-loss to the entry point.

Now you can be confident that your trade is profitable. If things get worse and the market sees a rapid deterioration, your stop-loss is already at the entry point. In the worst scenario, this will only bring your trade back to zero with no loss.

Following the 2% rule and raising the stop-loss increases your chances of success in trading

When you take on a trade, place your stop-loss somewhere below the entry point (in an uptrend). When you see that the trend is going up nicely, you should raise your stop-loss to the entry point. By doing this, even when there is a strong sell-off, you don't make money, but you also avoid a loss.

Take a look at the British pound/Japanese yen (GBP/JPY) four-hour chart below. After a retracement down to the 61.8% level, a long bullish candlestick formed, breaking the 50 SMA. You could place an entry upon the close of the marubozu candlestick, while the stop-loss could be placed just below the candlestick.

After several hours, the uptrend proves to be strong. After closing the first position at the 127% level, you could raise the stop-loss to the entry point. By doing this, you could ensure that the trade would at least break even.

If the trend continued in your expected direction, you might raise the stop-loss even more to make sure that your trade would certainly be closed with a profit.

As simple as it may seem, this technique can save you a lot of hard-earned money.

3. Develop the habit of using a trading plan

108

Unless you are a robot, you are subject to emotions of fear and greed, which will negatively affect your trading results. Any good trader should be able to define how they engage with the market, how they enter and exit trades. However, you can easily be affected by negative emotions.

A trading plan's purpose is to remove those emotions so that you can achieve the best state of mind as well as the best discipline in trading. As Benjamin Franklin said, "*If you fail to plan, you plan to fail.*" For every trader who is looking for a 'secret' in trading or for an edge in trading, this is what they need. Unless you have a detailed and clearly defined trading plan and you seriously stick to it, you cannot achieve long-term success in the financial market.

Most people have heard this at some time during their trading career. Nearly every trading course emphasizes the need for a trading plan. However, most people don't plan in a written form even once. They are simply not planning people.

A trading plan is a specific set of rules and guidelines that cover every aspect of your trading, including (but not limited to) your entry and exit, stop-loss, position size, risk amount, risk/reward ratio, trade management, and trading psychology.

By overcoming the two most dangerous emotions (greed and fear), you can have better control of your trading performance, making necessary adjustments to take your trading to the next levels.

Without a trading plan, you won't have an idea of how your trades perform during the whole process. You won't be able to distinguish between where you are doing well and where you need to improve.

To sum up, becoming a successful trader entails using a trading plan to plan your trade as well as to control yourself and your emotions. We've covered many strategies in this book in relation to entry, exit, stop-loss, risk/reward ratio, trade management, and more with Fibonacci retracements and extensions. However, unless you pre-define all of these elements in a plan and strictly follow them, chances are you will not apply those strategies effectively.

Click HERE to get a professionally designed trading plan for various types of trading.

Note: *In the google drive folder, make sure to login with your gmail account. Then, look for the bonus in connection with the book you are reading. As part of our efforts to overdeliver value to readers, you might notice the bonuses of other books you've not yet read there. Feel free to download them, too.*

4. The messages of a drawdown

Drawdown is the difference between the peak and the trough during a certain period of your trading. It is often quoted as the percentage of the decline above. For example, if a trading account has $20,000 in it, and the balance falls to $18,000 before recovering to $20,000, we'll say the account experienced a 10% drawdown.

Normal drawdown

A normal drawdown happens as a natural function of ups and downs of trading resulting from unexpected market conditions or small failures to follow your trading plan. It isn't treated as a real threat to your account, but should be well-managed to avoid becoming bigger than your tolerance, which may affect not only your trading account but also your emotions.

In the event of a normal drawdown, the first thing to do is re-checking your trading plan to make sure you are at least following the plan closely. If you're abiding by your trade rules, chances are that market conditions aren't conducive to your strategy at that time.

You may want to temporarily reduce your trade size even if the lost money is inconsiderable. Doing this, you can achieve a more objective view over the next market movements.

Problematic drawdown

This type of drawdown is more serious although it is not the end of the world. If handled appropriately, a trader can recover from the losses and gain back confidence shortly.

When undergoing a tough period when the loss hits your maximum tolerance, the first thing to do is to get out of the fire. Nothing is more necessary than stopping your trading at that time. It is often easier said than done because the market is always seducing you into putting more and more trades. Yet, once you've been successful in staying away from the trading desk for some time, at least you can reduce a lot of stress. To me, I often choose to stop trading when reaching a drawdown of 20% at least until the end of the month, depending on whether or not I've recovered the previous state of mind or not.

The next step is to pinpoint the causes of the drawdown. More often than not, it may result from many problems at the same time. However, you shouldn't try to resolve all of them at the same time. Instead, try to resort to the most severe problem which, from my experience, is often the failure to manage risks in trading. It could also be over-trading, impulsive trading, or any other causes that can lead to the drawdown. In any case, just stick to the most important problem until the situation is partly improved.

Also, you should reduce your trade size to help your better achieve an objective analysis standpoint of market fluctuations.

CHAPTER 11: BIG MISTAKES THAT MAY COST YOU A LOT OF MONEY

Fibonacci can tell you a lot about potential support/resistance zones and the correlation between buyers and sellers, if you use this powerful tool correctly. In contrast, any improper application of this technical tool may result in incorrect timing of the trade entry and exit, causing losses. In this chapter, I will pinpoint some mistakes to avoid when applying Fibonacci trading.

1. Expecting too much

One of the most common mistakes I have witnessed is that traders often expect certain things to happen so much that they seemed to be locked on some Fibonacci levels. It is the number one cause of anxiety, depression, and revenge trading.

For example, if you see an extension as a price target, you can become so obsessed with that level that you are unable to see other major support or resistance levels, or the strength of the trend to make the best of your trade. If you are looking for an entry, you become so confident in the price's bounce back from one level, only to see it break through without coming back.

You may easily think that the market has betrayed you. Fibonacci has betrayed you. You may forget that trading is all about probability. It needs a lot of practice and patience.

Therefore, if you are using Fibonacci as the core of your trading system, you should expect that it won't work around 30-40 percent of the time.

You can protect your capital during hard times via discipline and capital management, as discussed in the previous chapter. Please keep in mind that trading is not about right or wrong in any single trade. Trading is about how much you make through winning trades and how much you lose through losing trades **over a certain period of time.**

2. Using Fibonacci for short-term moves

As I mentioned in previous chapters, the volatility in short time frames (such as 5-minute, 15-minute, 30-minute, or even one-hour chart) is high, which can make Fibonacci signals inaccurate.

Shorter time frames make retracement levels less reliable since the market may not respect the support/resistance level on those time frames. Once the support/resistance levels are not respected, it won't be easy to use Fibonacci levels for determining entry and exit points.

Furthermore, shorter time frames may be presented with spikes, which can be attributed to the release of important economic/financial figures during the day. Such spikes can make it more difficult for traders to analyze the financial chart.

In general, regarding the technical indicators/ tools, the longer the observation is, the more reliable the data/figure is. This also applies to Fibonacci. Hence, applying Fibonacci tools in a longer time frame (i.e., at least the four-hour chart) is highly recommended to yield more positive results.

3. Inconsistency in the swing high and swing low used

When drawing Fibonacci retracements and extensions, it is advisable to use the reference points consistently. This means that the swing high and swing low should be referred to as shadow-to-shadow or body-to-body. As you can see, regarding examples in this book, I use the shadow to identify the swing high and swing low.

It may not work if you use the highest shadow as the swing high and the lowest closing price (lowest body) as a swing low and vice versa. This way, traders may find it hard to identify the most reliable support or resistance levels and pinpoint the correct timing of entry, stop-loss, and exit points.

The Australian and Canadian dollar (AUD/CAD) chart below pictures this error. The use of the candle wick at the top and the lower body of the candlestick at the bottom of the trend results in a mistaken identification of the resistance levels. Look how the price moved between the 23.6 percent level and the 38.2 percent level without picking up a major level as a correction point.

On the chart below, I use the wick of the candlestick for both swing high and swing low identification. You can see the Fibonacci retracements provide valuable insights into where the correction might lose steam (the 38.2 percent level), paving the way for a short entry.

4. Rely wholly on Fibonacci tools

Technically speaking, trading based on Fibonacci tools alone may not be considered a "mistake" like some of the points above. In many cases, you can ignore other tools, define entry and exit points just based on Fibonacci retracements and extensions, and still yield great results.

However, it is advisable to combine Fibonacci with other tools to enhance the reliability of market signals. I mentioned confirmation signals in many chapters in this book. Confirmation signals can be sought via other tools such as candlestick patterns, trend lines, moving averages, Elliott waves, etc. The more signals you have, the more positive potential your trade will have. Always remember that the market constantly changes, with lots of volatilities and turbulence. Combining more than one tool (but not too many) in your technical analysis will put the odds in your favor.

The gold daily chart below indicated a bullish trend. It was clear that there was a correction up to the 50 percent retracement level. Notice that the 50 SMA coincided with the 50 percent Fibonacci level, forming a powerful confluence there.

One more signal that would trigger an entry is the marubozu candlestick bouncing from the 50 SMA. The price maintained a bullish momentum afterward. Next, let's find the potential profit-taking target in this situation. Take a look at the next moves in the picture below.

The upward move was super strong until the 161.8 percent level, where strong volatilities occurred. As a conservative trader, you can choose to close your position here.

Also, we can see how the 161.8 percent level became such a hard support after it was broken as a resistance level. A more aggressive trader may opt for the three-part method on closing trades, aiming at a higher profit-taking price since the bulls were still so strong at the 161.8 percent level.

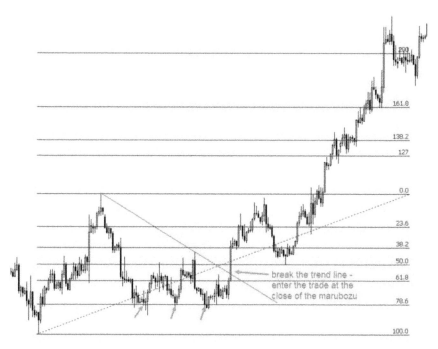

Example 2. Euro/US Dollar (EUR/USD) on the four-hour chart

In the example above, the price touched the 78.6 percent level a number of times without bouncing back, which may cause considerable confusion for traders.

In that case, using a trend line could be the perfect solution to the problem. Once again, a long bullish marubozu candlestick appeared, breaking the trend line and pushing the price much higher. With the stop-loss put just below the marubozu candlestick and a profit-taking target set at the 161.8 percent level, you could easily enjoy a 1:3 risk/reward ratio.

Example 3. US Dollar/Japanese Yen (USD/JPY) on the four-hour chart

This example is a great combination of Fibonacci and Elliott waves.

In this case, Wave 3 is the extended wave, with an extension level at the 261.8 percent line. Notice how the price reacted strongly at the end of Wave 3, which coincided with the 261.8 percent Fibonacci extension level.

Wave 2 is opposite to Wave 4 in terms of correction forming. While the former is deep and simple, the latter looked shallow and complex.

You can also ride Wave 5, though not as long as Wave 3. If you remember, the target of the last wave should be between 38.2 percent and 61.8 percent (Fibonacci expansions) of the distance from Wave 1 to Wave 3, calculated from the end of Wave 4. As you can see from the picture, a close of the position around 38.2 percent level would have helped catch most of the move.

APPENDIX: HOW TO SET UP FIBONACCI RETRACEMENTS AND EXTENSIONS

The following are some tips if you choose to use the MetaTrader trading platform to identify and guide your trades using Fibonacci.

1. **How to draw Fibonacci retracements and extensions in MetaTrader**

- Select the Fibonacci retracement tool from the quick menu:

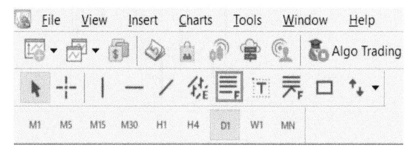

- If you cannot find it, go to the upper menu (**Insert**), click **Fibonacci,** and then select **Retracement**.
- Draw the retracement lines from the swing low to the swing high (in an uptrend) and from the swing high to the swing low (in a downtrend).

- Select them so that the lines going from 0 to 100 are highlighted.
- Click the right mouse button and select the first option - **Fibo properties**.
- In a new window, go to the second tab - **Fibo levels**. This is where you can add, remove, or edit your Fibonacci levels. To edit the value, just double-click on it.

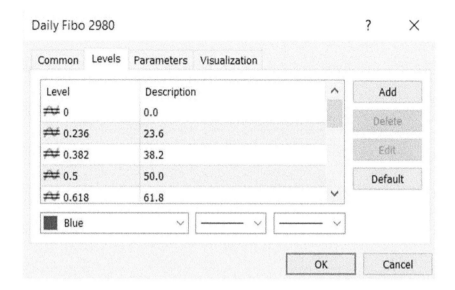

The first column in the table (**Level**) is a place where you define the levels. The second column (**Description**) indicates the description which will be shown on the chart.

Below are the most popular levels that I often use:

Level	Description
0	0
0.236	23.6
0.382	38.2
0.5	50.0
0.618	61.8
0.786	78.6
1	100
-0.27	127
-0.382	138.2
-0.618	161.8
-1	200

-1.618	261.8

Using this trick, you will have both retracement and extension levels

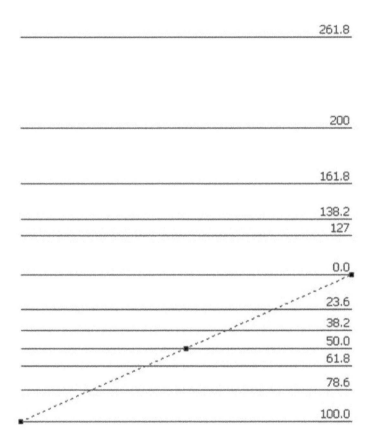

displayed simultaneously.

You may edit these levels if you want. To me, this is more than enough for analyzing your trades.

In a downtrend, when you look for a short opportunity, you draw the retracement **from the swing high (A) to the swing low (B):**

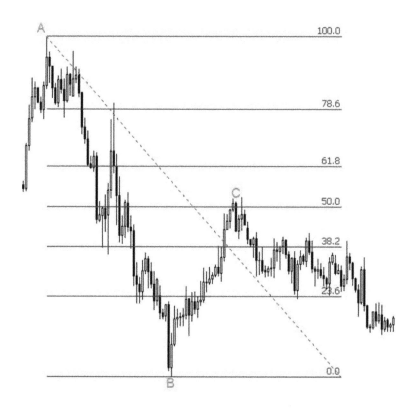

At point A, there will be the 100 percent Fibonacci level. Meanwhile, point B lies at the 0 percent Fibonacci level.

In an uptrend, when you look for a long opportunity, you draw the retracement **from the swing low (A) to the swing high (B):**

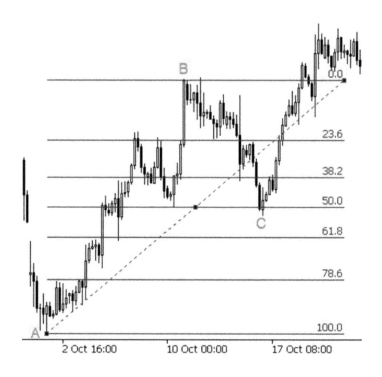

In such case, at point A, there will be the 100 percent Fibonacci level while point B lies at the 0 percent Fibonacci level.

2. How to draw Fibonacci expansions in MetaTrader

Let's take a downtrend as an example. Things are identical in an uptrend.

Click on the Fibonacci expansions tool symbol.

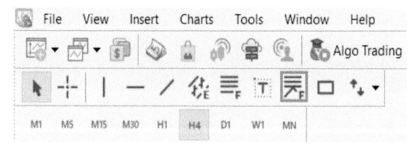

Next, click at the swing high, and one small spot appears (point A).

Do the same at the swing low (point B), and both points are automatically connected.

From point B, hold and drag the cursor to the correction point—C.

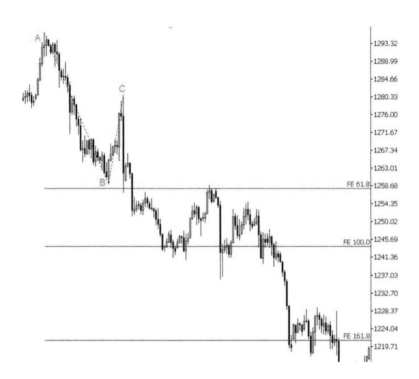

Milton Keynes UK
Ingram Content Group UK Ltd.
UKHW021207111224
3564UKWH00033B/97